THE ORGANIC FRUIT AND VEGETABLE GARDENER'S YEAR

KU-020-207

THE ORGANIC FRUIT AND VEGETABLE GARDENER'S YEAR

a seasonal guide to growing what you eat

Graham Clarke

GUILD OF MASTER
CRAFTSMAN PUBLICATIONS

First published in 2008 by
Guild of Master Craftsman Publications Ltd
Castle Place, 166 High Street,
Lewes, East Sussex BN7 1XU

Text © Graham Clarke, 2008
© in the Work GMC Publications Ltd, 2008

Reprinted 2009, 2011

All photographs taken by the author except those
listed on the following pages:
www.morguefile.com: 22 (bottom right), 23, 24, 25,
28, 34 (top right), 42 (bottom left), 66 (bottom left), 93
(bottom right), 102, 103 (bottom right), 118, 125
(bottom), 136 (bottom) and 140; Hozelock: 30, 70 (top),
Mr Fothergill's seeds: 56 (top), 90 (top);
Virginia Brehaut: 71 (right)

Illustrations by Michelle Willeter

ISBN 978-1-86108-566-5

All rights reserved

The right of Graham Clarke to be identified as the author
of this work has been asserted in accordance with the
Copyright, Designs and Patents Act 1988, sections 77
and 78.

No part of this publication may be reproduced, stored in
a retrieval system or transmitted in any form or by any
means without the prior permission of the publisher and
copyright owner.

This book is sold subject to the condition that all designs
are copyright and are not for commercial reproduction
without the permission of the designer and copyright
owner.

The publishers and author can accept no legal
responsibility for any consequences arising from the
application of information, advice or instructions given in
this publication.

A catalogue record for this book is available from the
British Library.

Production Manager: Jim Bulley
Publisher: Jonathan Bailey
Managing Editor: Gerrie Purcell
Editor: Virginia Brehaut
Editorial Assistant: Hedda Roennevig
Managing Art Editor: Gilda Pacitti
Designer: Chloë Alexander

Set in Impact, Nofret and Helvetica Neue

Colour origination by GMC Reprographics
Printed and bound in China by Hing Yip Printing Co. Ltd.

Contents

Organic basics

Spring

Autumn

Summer

Information

Winter

How to use this book

Organic basics

introduces the main
principles of organics
with some handy ideas
of how to get started
as an organic kitchen
gardener.

Tips & tasks appears at the beginning of each
season section to show which general jobs need
to be done at that time of year.

Go to this alphabetical section for non-specific
advice; for example, how to protect plants in
winter.

Fruit, vegetables and herb listings

Easy-reference alphabetical listings of fruit, vegetables and herbs.

Symbol indicators

to show at a glance which tasks need to be done. See key below for symbol meanings.

Small garden tips

give ideas to those gardeners who don't have much space.

Organic tips

give you extra hints on how to achieve great organic results.

Key to symbol indicators

 Pruning

 Harvesting

 Feeding

 Weeds, pests & diseases

 Planting out

 Propagation

 Plant protection & support

 Soil preparation & cultivation

Watering

Introduction

BITING into your first strawberry of the year is a joy like no other! The mouth drools at the thought of the juiciest tomatoes, the sweetest dessert apples, the raspberries in summer pudding – then there are the flavoursome peas and beans, the tangy members of the onion family and the wholesome and health-giving members of the brassica family!

For many gardeners with a bit of space, growing their own fruits and vegetables can become a bit of an obsession. And these days increasing numbers of gardeners want this 'from-the-plant-to-the-table' freshness to go hand-in-hand with sound organic and environmentally conscious principles. But can you possibly achieve the best of the former and still fully embrace and adopt the latter? I reckon you can.

Most amateur gardeners like the thought of being 'organic', and usually they start off in the right way. But as with anyone giving up a habit, such as smoking or alcohol, giving up the use of garden chemicals is not easy: the first sighting of a slug and the temptation to get the latest off-the-shelf convenience poison can be all-consuming.

To be really organic, however, you should remove the offending pests by hand and dispatch them humanely. If the infestation is severe, you might even resort to an approved, environmentally friendly pesticide that has been created from plant extract. Introducing some predatory wasps, mites, nematodes and bacterium can be a most efficient and sensible control, too. Yes, there are always organic alternatives to garden chemicals, and I implore every gardener to try them.

Pick up any old volume on fruit or vegetable growing, and you will see that masses of advice is given to the plethora of pests and diseases that are likely to infect and infest the crops. These bugs and ailments are attracted to home food crops perhaps more than any other garden plant group, so if you are not wanting to take the easy way out and use chemicals, it is important to know how to grow the finest plants in terms of health. The healthier the plant, the better able it is to resist being infected.

I believe that traditional chemical-using gardeners should take a year off from using them. Try existing for 12 months without using any form of conventional man-made chemical poisons, and see what happens. Yes, there may be a few more pests and diseases around. And yes, there may be the odd fruit or stalk that should be discarded. But watchfulness, prompt removal of offenders and, of course, the desire to protect the environment are strong weapons in the war, and the satisfaction you'll get from growing something fantastic, without leaving a dirty great carbon (or poisonous) footprint on the world in doing so, is extremely liberating.

Essentially, this book is a compilation of my columns from the magazine *Healthy & Organic Living*. These have been expanded, updated and reorganized so that they form a comprehensive year calendar for the organic fruit and vegetable gardener. Contained within is information on all the growing processes, from variety choice and good cultivation, through to solving problems and even how to harvest your plants in the optimum way.

The aims of this book are twofold: first, to set any conventional gardener wanting to grow their own food on the right course to becoming 'organic'; and second, to serve as a reminder to existing environmentalists that fruits and vegetables need quite specific attention if they are to be grown in the optimum way organically. I've never seen organic advice presented in such a way, and I'm personally delighted with the modern, concise and easy-to-follow style. I hope you will be also.

Graham Clarke, 2008

Organ

**Attracting wildlife
to your garden** 25

**Sourcing local plants
and seeds** 28

Watering wisely 30

cBasics

Garden compost

All gardeners should learn to recycle their garden waste by composting. The end result of all your hard work will be a wonderful, friable, dark, fine material that can be dug into the soil, used as a mulch or even used as a seed compost.

ANY plant matter can be used on the compost heap when it has become too old or been dug up. It will rot down to a fraction of its former size, and in so doing will become good, available humus off which other plants can grow. You can include peelings and unused bits of vegetables from the kitchen, as well as grass mowings, shredded prunings and any other bits of soft, green matter. Even small amounts of shredded paper can be added.

Prunings need to be shredded as trees and shrubs that have been pruned are very woody, and wood takes a long time to rot. However, the smaller the woody bits the quicker they'll rot. Soft things are best for a compost heap, so the rule is: the harder the material, the smaller it should be. A good heap should rot in the quickest way, so do not put too much wood in/on, even if the wood is shredded. The secret to making good compost is the 'little-and-often' principle. You should aim for a really good mixture of things.

▼ **Create a fine, fertile soil by making compost and your plants will be much stronger and healthier.**

▲ **Soft plant material and kitchen vegetable scraps are the essential ingredients for a good compost heap.**

Material to avoid

What should NOT go on to a compost heap?

ASIDE from general household rubbish such as plastics, metals and glass, more or less anything else can. It is not advisable, however, to add cooked food – meat, fish, cheese and grease. Apart from smelling bad (rotting meat and dairy food smells completely different to rotting raw vegetable matter), you could be encouraging rats and other unwanted vermin. Also, don't add the roots of perennial weeds such as couch grass, ground elder, bindweed, docks and dandelions. These will almost certainly continue to grow and you'll end up spreading them around the garden.

Getting started

A COMPOST heap should be positioned directly on to the ground. A heap (or an enclosure) about 3ft (1m) square at the base and 4ft (1.2m) high should be suitable for most gardens. The

▲ **An open 'pen' compost heap can create some excellent compost – and in huge quantities.**

area should be enclosed by some kind of mesh to prevent the contents from spilling out on to the surrounding area. You can either buy a ready-made bin from the garden centre or simply knock together four upright posts and encircle them with chicken wire (see box below). The edges will become dry and will take longer to rot, but inside the heap things should rot down nicely.

Build up the heap in 6in (15cm) layers of garden or kitchen waste. It is a good idea to water each layer, to help the decomposing process. Making good compost can take as little as six weeks, if it is the height of summer and you add just small bits of green matter and some activator

Types of bin

I've used many different styles of compost bin and have concluded that the best type is a simple rigid wire mesh container. If you have a shop-bought compost bin it will already have a lid, but if you have an open 'pen' affair then you should really cover the compost each time you add something – a piece of old carpet is ideal. This stops the top layer from drying out, but during cold weather it also acts as insulation. I also fix black plastic or wooden panels to the sides to stop the freeze from entering the sides of the heap.

Diseased plant material

Apart from the materials to avoid (see main text), the following diseased vegetable matter should not be added to a compost heap:

• Members of the cabbage family suffering with club root disease

• Onions suffering from white rot

• Potato foliage suffering from blight

• Potato tubers and roots from eelworm-infected plants

– usually a nitrogen–based substance that speeds up the rotting process. Or it can take a year or more, if there are lots of thick, dry autumn leaves, or a fair amount of shredded wood, or you started the heap in the autumn (the speed of rotting decreases in winter). You can also create your own leafmould by laying down rotted leaves, collected together and compressed over several years. These rot into a bulky organic mass, which adds fibre to the soil, improves drainage and helps to retain moisture.

▼ **Modern, contained compost bins usually have a sliding door front for easy removal of the contents.**

Peat and its alternatives

The gardening world is so entrenched in the use of peat that the issue of whether we should or shouldn't use it is a complex one.

ENVIRONMENTALLY, most keen gardeners know that peat is a natural resource that takes thousands of years to renew, and that we should try to use less of it. Equally, many experienced, knowledgeable gardeners say that peat is by far the best of the available 'growing media', and the so-called peat alternatives are not as good if you want to grow the best plants.

It is true that in the past the alternatives to peat gave disappointing results. Flowers were fewer and smaller, and plants appeared to be weaker. But much has been done to improve this, and today the peat alternatives are very much better and have performed well in trials. It is always worth asking yourself whether or not you actually need to use compost. Many crops can be sown directly into the ground and it is also possible to create highly successful potting mixes from your own garden compost.

What is peat?

IN cool, wet climates the amount of water that falls is very high, and the rate of evaporation is low. Deposits of vegetable matter tend to remain wet for long periods, and surface water gathers in undrained hollows. Under these conditions vegetable matter does not decompose so readily, and over many years tends to accumulate as peat.

▲ An area of wetland where the vegetable matter does not decompose readily and accumulates as peat is known as a 'peat bog'.

On higher land the wet, unrotted peat may form a layer several feet thick, and this is known as 'blanket bog', historically formed mainly from sphagnum moss and deer grass. In poorly drained hollows, vegetable matter accumulates below water level and gradually the deposit fills with water, forming 'basin peat'. The peat is raised above water level by a raised growth of moss.

Using peat vs avoiding peat

THERE is an on-going debate amongst gardeners over whether peat is renewable or not. Many gardening experts are adamant that it is and, even more, that its extraction does much to help peoples of some of the poorer nations.

◀ The benefits and drawbacks of using peat-based compost causes much discussion between gardeners.

Take, for example, Lithuania – a country with widespread poverty. The people there depend on the peat industry and the country produces some of the world's finest peat.

However, the argument that peat is not sustainable, as it takes thousands of years to renew itself, is also compelling. As a habitat, wetland areas (from where peat is extracted) support many rare and vulnerable plant and animal species. Peat bogs also act as carbon stores, and it is thought that they are playing a useful role in reducing the impact of global climate change.

There are still problems with some of the alternatives. For example, coir – the fibre from coconuts taken during industrial processing – comes from the Far East and Indonesia. The retrieval, processing and transportation of coir fibre has a huge global impact in itself. For me, environmental benefits of 'home–grown' in terms of sustainability, reduced food miles and general impact outweigh the occasional need for small quantities of peat.

The more one debates the use of peat or its alternatives, the deeper entrenched one becomes. At the end of it all, the choice has to belong to you, the gardener.

▼ **Cross-section of a peat bog. This one is almost 10ft (3m) deep.**

Peat alternatives

Collectively, amateur gardeners use far more peat than professional horticulturalists, and there is plenty of scope for using more of the alternatives listed below.

Coir
This is a coarse fibre from the coconut palm. As well as carpets and brushes, it is increasingly being used to make peat substitute. For composts the cork-like substance found between the larger fibres is extracted, and it is used most successfully in the commercial growing of roses, bulbs and tomatoes.

Bark
Mainly from renewable conifers and pines, this is available from large pieces to fine compost. Some producers claim that bark can act as a complete replacement for peat without any loss of quality.

Woodfibre
This is created from waste wood and is heat and high-pressure air treated to open up the fibres and prevent it from retaining nitrogen. It is mainly added as a bulking agent to reduced peat composts.

Green waste
The godfather of them all, it has been found that 'green waste' can contain micro-organisms that actually inhibit or suppress plant diseases. Any plant residue from weeds, grass, dead plants, prunings, vegetable waste – even sawdust and newsprint – can be made into compost, and commercial businesses that are springing up are doing this on a large scale.

Chemical-free weed control

New organic 'converts' are often concerned as to how they will control pests, disease and especially weeds without using chemicals.
It's not such a big step to take as there is much that can be done.

▲ **A sea of weeds – in this case perennial thistles – will spread to cultivated ground fast. When removing such weeds, ensure that all roots are pulled up.**

GOOD gardening practices are by far and away the best method to prevent pests and diseases. This means good soil cultivation (in order to grow strong, healthy plants) and good 'hygiene' (that is, weed control in order to prevent the sorts of plants that are the breeding or feeding grounds of many pests and diseases). Many types will become host plants for the breeding of aphids, and others make ideal homes for fungal diseases such as mildew and rust. Weeds are also plants that compete with our cultivated plants for light, moisture and nutrition from the soil.

When you are first setting out plants in your kitchen garden, you should make sure that the ground is completely weed–free. Weeds fall into two main categories. The first are the annuals, which propagate themselves by seeding from the mature plants, and which only last one year. Then there are the perennials, which spread by the roots and shoots that creep along the ground, and which persist from year to year. Perennials also set seed and propagate themselves.

The easiest weeds to control are annuals, which are best kept in check organically by hoeing and mulching. The perennial weeds, such as ground elder, couch grass (or twitch), bindweed, docks, thistles and perennial nettles, will need to be dug out and completely removed from the soil by hand, making sure to pull up all the roots.

Mulching

ESSENTIALLY, a mulch is a layer of organic (preferably, although horticultural fabrics and plastics may also be used) material applied around plants and on top of the soil surface. In addition to suppressing weed growth, there are other benefits in putting down a 2in (5cm) layer of mulch spread over a warmed, moist soil in spring. Preventing evaporation from the soil is another. And a third benefit is that the mulch will gradually add to the soil humus content through the action of earthworms.

▲ **Small beds can be kept free of weeds by regular hand-weeding, without the need to walk over the soil.**

What are the materials to use for mulching? Homemade composts and leafmould are full of plant goodness and are certainly the easiest of products to get hold of – or make yourself. Farmyard manure is also excellent, but a ready supply is not so easily sourced. Again, these

▼ **Cocoa shell can be used to keep weeds down – and will even make the border smell of chocolate for a short while.**

materials should be applied when they are well rotted. If applied in a raw state, then their composite strength (acidic and high in ammonia) could damage the soil or any live plant material it touches. In fact, even in its well–rotted state, it should not be laid so that it touches the plants, as it will cause 'burning'.

Bark is relatively cheap, light and biodegradable and also has excellent weed–suppressing and moisture-retaining qualities. The disadvantage to using bark is that it needs topping up most years, and its appearance is not always to everyone's taste. It is, however, an excellent surface for pathways, and is safe for children.

Cocoa bean shells, coir fibre and even hair mulches are available. There are also a number of different fabric mulches for allowing rain through, but preventing (or at least reducing) water evaporation from the soil.

Stone mulches are long lasting and there is a huge range of colours and size grades to choose from. The disadvantages to using them, however, are worth noting. To start with, in the autumn when leaves fall it is difficult to sweep or clear the area. A thin layer of gravel will afford some moisture retention in the soil, but to do this effectively the layer should be thick – 3in (7.5cm) or more. No matter how thick a gravel mulch, weeds will always seem to germinate in it, but fortunately they are usually quite easy to remove. It is advisable, no essential, to lay down a weed–preventing membrane (widely available from garden centres) before putting down the chips. A popular alternative to natural yellowish or brown gravel is chipped slate, in shades of blue, grey or plum.

Ground cover

GROUND–COVER plants grow along the ground, smothering weeds in their wake. They can, in an ideal situation, cover every bit of available soil so that you can't see the bare earth (if you can, it means that weeds can grow there too). Ground coverers are the perfect choice if you have an awkward bank of soil that is difficult to grass over (as it makes mowing dangerous) and if you have dryish soil in shade, such as under a tree. They are also the perfect choice if you have a large area and little time to look after it – for these plants, in general, look after themselves.

They may be herbaceous, shrubby, woody, succulent or grass–like. Ground–cover plants may be clumping, sprawling or vining. They may be evergreen (the most useful), or they can be deciduous or somewhere in between. And they may also be annual, biennial or perennial.

For the most part, ground–cover plants can be anywhere between 1in (2.5cm) and 4ft (1.2m) high, and you can choose from boring green types, to those that are really quite vibrant and colourful.

Here are six of the best:

Bergenia (elephant's ears): Reaching some 12in. (30cm) high, the leaves are thick, leathery, shiny and evergreen. They turn purplish bronze in the autumn and can be quite red in winter. The flowers are heads of bright pink in mid–spring.

Erica and **Calluna** (heather): Everyone knows what heathers look like. Trouble is they mostly need an acid soil and not everyone can provide this. The three I like to recommend are 'King George' (deep rose–pink flowers), 'Springwood White' (white flowers) and 'Vivelli' (almost blood–red flowers, with dark green foliage that becomes bronzy in winter).

Geranium (cranesbill): The 'true' geraniums (not the summer bedding and pot–grown pelargoniums) are excellent for dry soils, and for edging pathways and growing on slopes.

Hosta (plantain lily): Here we come to a plant that is grown in gardens everywhere, but people don't necessarily think of it as a ground coverer. Although it doesn't spread indefinitely like some of the others I'm including, *Hosta* has such large leaves that a clump of them growing together can provide really dense cover. Again, there are dozens (nay, hundreds it seems) to choose from – go for a leaf style you like.

▲ **Using a Dutch hoe is the best way to control weeds between rows of plants – but avoid damaging roots near to the soil surface.**

Juniperus (juniper): There are several forms that have lovely dense foliage and grow in a prostrate habit. I used to grow one next to a manhole cover. Branches came over the cover and hid the ugliness of it; you just had to move the branches aside to get in to the drains.

Osteospermum: This daisy plant from South Africa must have a sunny spot. Other than that it will grow in practically any soil, doesn't mind being dry and rewards with fabulous flowers for most of the summer. Many forms exist with flowers in shades from white through pinks and creams to mauve and purple.

Organic war on weeds

Here are some non-chemical ways to keep your patch free of weeds:

● Hoeing is the most efficient method of controlling annual weeds in the veg garden and shrub border. Push the blade of the hoe through the top layer of soil – this will cut through the weeds just under the surface.

● Mulch to suppress weed growth, but make sure that the ground is clear of perennial weeds before it is applied.

● Keep a special look out for free-seeding bittercress, groundsel and willow herb. If one of these runs to seed, you'll have hundreds in a few weeks.

● Don't fork through the soil around plants during spring and summer, as this will turn up a fresh supply of weed seeds to germinate.

● Perennial weeds have deep roots that should be dug out carefully to limit re-growth. Remove every piece of small fibrous roots of such weeds as ground elder and bindweed.

Companion planting

Some plants, when grown together, can mutually benefit each other whether it be by repelling common pests, or just by giving a bit of shade. Organic gardeners make the most of this with some clever planting.

▲ Tomatoes seem to grow better if marigolds are grown nearby, as these flowers deter whitefly.

GOOD organic gardening (and farming, for that matter) relies not just on the avoidance of chemicals, and the more diligent use of environmentally sound products. It is also based on the study of (and an expanding knowledge about) the mutual influences of living organisms. Among these are root excretions, and other organic substances present in leaves and roots, or certain odours, insect–repelling or attracting substances, biotic compounds, and so on. Thus, individual plants can, and do, have specific influences on other plants around them, and on the micro–life in the soil.

In its simplest form, one tall–growing plant gives shade, thus temporarily helping – or suppressing – another plant nearby. Also, plants may interact simply in competing for water, light, nutrients and air. The following, therefore, is just a small example of how choosing to grow certain plants can have a beneficial – or detrimental – affect on others. And as this does not require the use of man–made or high–energy compounds, adopting 'companion planting' is a perfect form of gardening for the organic enthusiast.

Good companions A to Z

Asparagus Grow this next to tomatoes (or grow tomatoes 'between' asparagus crowns). A substance named asparagin, which is given off by asparagus roots, helps to control some of the soil pests that affect tomatoes.

▼ French marigolds – and all forms of *Tagetes* – excrete a substance from their roots which kills nematode pests.

Beetroot These appear to grow well near to dwarf beans, onions and kohlrabi; and they seem to assist the development of lettuce and cabbage.

Cabbages One of the main pests of the cabbage family is the white cabbage butterfly, and this may be repelled by the following plants growing near the cabbages: tomatoes, celery, sage, rosemary, thyme, mint, hyssop and various forms of *Artemesia* (the southernwood genus).

Carrots The carrot fly is the most troublesome of pests; it is the caterpillar of this fly that attacks the young roots of growing plants. It often pupates in mature stored carrots. Various other vegetables and plants have been found to be repellents: try onions and leeks and strong–smelling herbs such as rosemary, sage and wormwood. In fact, some gardeners sow carrots and leeks together in the same row (at the ratio of 2 parts leek to 3 parts carrot). The carrots will be ready to harvest early, which gives the leeks time to mature before autumn.

French marigolds These excrete a substance from their roots which kills nematodes (pests of many plants, including potatoes and roses). Tomatoes seem to grow better if French marigolds are grown nearby, and it has long been known that the presence of the marigolds deters the presence of white fly, particularly in greenhouses.

Leeks When sown in alternate rows, leeks and celery (or celeriac) do very well together. The slender leeks grow well between the bushier others; both are potassium lovers, and both do well on goat and pig manure.

Lettuce Because it is such a favourite, much has been learnt about lettuce over the past century. For instance, it likes to grow with strawberries, is aided by the presence of carrots nearby, and it seems to make radishes tender in summer. Early lettuce in good soil seems to aid onions.

Mice The everlasting pea (*Lathyrus latifolius*), spearmint (*Mentha spicata*) and the spurges (*Euphorbia lathyrus* and *E. lactea*) have a reputation for repelling field mice, moles and other rodents.

▲ **Nasturtiums are attractive, easy summer flowers in their own right and can be used to deter blackfly.**

Nasturtiums It is widely experienced that nasturtiums planted near to broccoli keep the latter free from blackfly and greenfly. If apple trees are surrounded by several nasturtium plants, woolly aphids are repelled.

Nut trees Most types, but especially the walnut (*Juglans* spp) repel stable flies, houseflies and flies that live on cattle. Nut trees in pastures, therefore, can be a great comfort to cattle and horses. Such trees, if near manure piles (and entrances to barns and stables) may reduce significantly the number of flies present.

Sweetcorn This does well with early potatoes; and sweetcorn development is aided by beans and peas that put back nitrogen into the soil which it uses up. Beans, on the other hand, can benefit from the slight shade given by the corn plants. And a row of dill on either side of sweet corn seems to make both plants grow larger and stronger.

Bad companions A to Z

Apples These should not be stored with potatoes or carrots, as the apples lose their flavour. The potatoes do not keep well, and the carrots take on a bitter flavour.

Fennel This strongly flavoured herb hinders the germination of caraway and coriander, and disturbs the growth of dwarf beans and tomatoes.

Grass Root tip growth of apples and pears can be suppressed by the root excretions of grass. In other words, apple and pear trees will grow better under open cultivation.

Kohlrabi This member of the cabbage family has a harmful effect on tomatoes, and it grows poorly near runner beans.

▼ **Sunflowers planted nearby to potatoes are said to stunt the growth of both plants.**

Peas These are inhibited by onions, garlic and shallots.

Pine Rain washing down over pine–needles contains secretions which have a deleterious effect upon the germination of seeds. Pine needles and shoots decomposing in soil noticeably inhibits the growth of beneficial soil bacteria, particularly if the soil is acidic. Do not site open compost heaps under pine (or other conifers) as the litter and residue from these conifers holds back the rotting processes.

Potatoes Nearby sunflowers will cause both types of plant to be stunted. Potatoes in the vicinity of birch trees tend to rot more readily. Root excretions from potatoes somewhat inhibit growth of tomatoes. Pumpkins, also, grow poorly when next to potatoes. And if potatoes are growing close to raspberries they seem to be more susceptible to blight.

Raspberries should not be grown in amongst blackberries as neither crop will do well.

Rue This pungent herb, *Ruta graveolens*, should not be grown with sweet basil (*Ocimum* spp) as neither will do well.

Runner beans These are suppressed if grown next to onions; whilst beetroot and kohlrabi both grow poorly near to runner beans.

Tomatoes These give off root excretions which have an inhibitory effect on the growth of young apricot trees. It has also been found that potatoes grown near tomatoes were not resistant to potato blight. And tomatoes do not grow well if kohlrabi and fennel are growing nearby.

Walnuts Members of the *Juglans* genus have an inhibiting effect upon the growth of tomatoes and potatoes.

Attracting wildlife to your garden

Attracting wildlife to your garden or plot makes sound organic sense. Pollinators, predators and microscopic composters are vital for a balanced, organic cycle helping your plot to look after itself.

THERE is plenty of animal life that chirps, swoops, pecks, forages, snuffles and shuffles in our gardens during the year. There are two main reasons why such creatures visit our gardens, and these are food and shelter. So, what can we do to attract more wildlife to the garden?

Food

IF you encourage insects (which are at the bottom of the food chain) to the garden, you will be encouraging, insect–eating mammals and birds, which in turn encourages the larger

mammals. So start by making sure you are growing plenty of flowering plants (see panels on pages 26 and 27). There is always some insect activity – even in winter with some forms of moth, fly, beetle, even bee – and these will all make use of flower nectar.

Similarly, invertebrates such as worms and slugs are great food for hedgehogs and many birds. Whereas I don't think we want to encourage slugs, doing things in the garden that promotes the growth of the worm population will benefit everyone. And this means having good soil. Digging the ground once a year, and applying compost and manure to a garden will

▼ **Honey bees provide a valuable service, pollinating flowers and encouraging fruits to form.**

▼ **Butterflies (this is a brightly coloured monarch) are a fascinating and welcome addition to the garden scene.**

▲ **Small birds will feed on many types of garden plant, but need extra food (such as seeds and nuts) in winter.**

improve the soil – and improve life for worms. With a hedgehog or two in your garden, it is unlikely you will ever have too big a problem with slugs, for the prickly mammals eagerly seek out and consume the slimy gastropods. You can put out food for hedgehogs (just an occasional bowl of dog food). Foxes (if you don't mind them), badgers and woodmice will appreciate meat bones, poultry leftovers, peanuts, apple cores or tinned dog food put out at dusk. These foods could also encourage rodents, so you need to keep an eye out and stop supplying the food if you know that rats are a problem. It is almost inevitable that rats will turn up in your garden every now and again, and the occasional visit should not be cause to worry. However, when they decide to stay and breed, this is when problems can occur.

Shelter

SANCTUARY and cover is provided in plenty by gardens with shrubberies and sheds, trees and (increasingly) trampolines. Wildlife frequently prefers the fenced and walled seclusion of domestic gardens rather than the open fields or dangerous woodlands where predators can get at them more easily.

Plants for bees and butterflies

Friendly insect life is at its most active in the summer. Bees and butterflies are flitting from flower to flower like mad things. The best way to attract them is to grow the plants that these insects either feed or breed on.

For butterflies, you can't do better than *Buddleja davidii*. But they also like bugle (*Ajuga reptans*), flowering currant (*Ribes sanguineum*), globe thistle (*Echinops bannaticus*), grape hyacinth (*Muscari armeniacum*), holly, honeysuckle, ivy, forms of *Calluna vulgaris*, *Sedum spectabile* (but not 'Brilliant' or 'Autumn Joy') and thyme, mint and lavender.

Bees also like all of the above, but they especially like rosemary and heathers, and the autumn-flowering Michaelmas daisies.

▼ **Buddleja davidii is known as the 'butterfly bush' owing to its popularity with all species of butterfly, which visit in search of nectar.**

▲ **Hedges make excellent habitats for insects, birds and small mammals.**

Make sure there is plenty of wildlife shelter available. This includes log piles, thick hedges for birds and dense shrubberies where lots of dry leaves on the ground can provide hibernating and resting places for hedgehogs. Take care when rummaging around the garden in winter to not disturb hibernating wildlife.

You can buy bird nesting boxes and bat boxes, houses for hedgehogs, toads and frogs, as well as beehives and lacewing logs. Just think about providing shelter and seclusion, and you won't go far wrong. Finally, make sure that ponds have escape routes for frogs and toads. These amphibians cannot get out of steep–sided ponds and will perish.

Attracting birds

It's important to keep garden birds well fed during winter. The number and variety of birds coming to a garden can be largely due to the type of food provided. Hanging bird feeders containing seeds, peanuts and specialist mixes will be good for the smaller species, such as greenfinches, sparrows and blue tits. A flat bird table will be better for robins, chaffinches and larger birds.

You can also encourage and satisfy birds by growing the types of plants from which they like to feed. Grow plants that are prolific producers of seed or berries, such as holly, cotoneaster and the colourful firethorns (*Pyracantha* spp).

The best environment for birds by far, is the hedgerow. If you have space, plant elder, rowan, dogwood and mountain ash. If not, just grow the guelder rose (*Viburnum opulus*) or silver birch.

Many flowers will provide seeds that can be collected and stored for use when the birds really need them. Good choices include poppy, forget-me-not, sunflower and foxglove. If you grow teasels, which keep their seedheads in winter, the birds can help themselves.

Sourcing local plants and seeds

These days many gardeners buy ready–germinated plants; but the trouble with this is that you don't know how many far they have travelled before you bought them and you cannot guarantee that they were grown organically.

Propagate your own plants

IF you have a greenhouse you can sow a huge range of fruit and vegetable seeds yourself, harden them off and then plant them out when conditions are suitable. If not, then there are still many varieties that can be sown directly outside straight into the ground. Organic seeds can be bought from garden centres or purchased by mail order. This book tells you which fruits, vegetables and herbs can be propagated at home, as well as how and when to do it.

▼ **Propagating your own plants is hugely satisfying, cheaper and you know about its growing process.**

Saving seed

YOU can save and use the seed from many kitchen garden plants, perennials and annuals. Collect the seed on a dry day, making sure they are not damp otherwise they may germinate or go mouldy. Transfer seeds to a clean, dry jar. Properly dried seeds will keep for several years at a steady, cool temperature (such as in the door of your fridge), in an airtight container. Do not keep them in the garden shed, as temperature fluctuations may wake them up.

▼ **Seeds can be saved from 'open-pollinated' plants – these are species that will come true to type when sown.**

Buy locally grown plants

BUYING young vegetable and bedding plants isn't the greenest way to garden, owing to the amount of energy required to mass-produce them. However, many garden centres are starting to promote 'locally grown' alternatives to cut down on the road miles. Couple this with the fact that the plants are growing in no-peat or reduced-peat compost, and you can be assured that you are doing what you can to reduce the environmental impact. Make sure new purchases are fully acclimatized before you plant them out. Take the trays into the open during the day, putting them under cover as night falls. Gradually leave the plants out for longer periods over a week or so, until you're confident they are hardened enough to plant out.

▲ **Many nurseries and garden centres are now promoting locally grown plants.**

Seed swapping

Look out in your local area for seed swapping events, which are becoming very popular. It is a great way to get hold of unusual varieties, find out which varieties grow well in your neighbourhood and swap tips and advice with other gardeners. Meeting up with other gardeners to discuss experiences, share 'best practice' and swap seeds cements a sense of community – and saves you money as well.

Apart from these feel-good factors, there are some sound environmental reasons why seed swapping is important. It keeps diversity of locally adapted varieties alive. It keeps 'seed making' in the garden and out of the laboratory. It helps protect biodiversity. By swapping seeds, age-old seed-sowing skills are maintained. This is not bad for something you can do in your back garden!

In the UK, the national association known as Garden Organic has a Heritage Seed Library, which aims to conserve and make available vegetable varieties that are not in general commerce. Over the decades many varieties have been dropped from popular seed catalogues, so this collection contains many of these but also some varieties that have never been in a catalogue. Similar associations in other countries can be found via the internet.

Don't forget to grow open-pollinating vegetable varieties (types that pollinate naturally, as opposed to man-made hybrids) so you can collect seed to re-sow and swap, and to protect plant biodiversity.

Watering wisely

No living thing can exist without water, and when it comes to rainfall we need to capture it. There are tanks, sumps and buckets… but water butts are the best for storing rainwater and therefore conserving our precious mains supply.

▲ **Watering should only be carried out in the evening, to avoid unnecessary evaporation.**

ESSENTIALLY, any large water container is best placed in a shaded area. It is not desirable for the water inside to be in the full glare of the sun as it will heat up – often to quite high temperatures. Because natural rainfall is collected via roofs, gutters and downpipes it has attracted a number of impurities on its travels. High temperatures can materially alter the content and chemical balance, and bacteria in the water can quickly grow. This is when the water will turn green, and perhaps start to smell badly.

An important consideration when siting water butts is to put them next to structures where there are gutters and, preferably, downpipes (otherwise you will need to install these as well). My three water butts are filled via water run–off from the house, the garage and the greenhouse. But you can place them anywhere else that provides similar run–off: annexes, sheds, outhouses, conservatories, car porch and so on.

Water-wise advice

My golden rules for saving water are:

• Catch as much rain water as possible – ring your local water authority and ask whether they offer special deals on water butts (and if they don't, ask them why not!)

• Watering should only be carried out in the evenings, so the water has time to soak into the soil where it can be used by the plant roots.

• Direct the water to the bases of the plants – don't waste it by spraying it over the leaves where much of it will evaporate.

• Use water–retaining granules – polymers – in containers; these absorb moisture, swell up and release it to plant roots when required. Some people use them in the open border for salad vegetables. These will help to conserve water in the soil or compost, thereby reducing the need to water so frequently.

• Sink funnels, made from cut–down plastic drinks bottles, alongside newly transplanted vegetables such as brassicas, tomatoes, celery, peas and beans. Filling these two or three times a day in hot weather will do a power of good, but you'll need a lot of bottles if the rows are long!

Finally, it would be remiss of me not to mention the soil at this stage. A garden created for the intelligent use of water MUST have a good soil, containing plenty of moisture–retaining humus. Whereas this is usually built up over months and years, there is actually no better time to start than when the garden is still a 'blank canvas'.

▼ **Large water tanks like this are perfect for greenhouses where you can submerge a watering can easily.**

Using 'grey water'

In times of drought it is not unusual to find gardeners using bath or shower water on their plants because, once cool, it is perfect for use in the garden. It is possible to store such domestic water when rainwater is no longer available. By fitting a diverting valve on the bath or shower outlet so that it can supply the garden water storage system, it is possible to supply cooled bath water direct to the roots of plants – at any time of the year.

The types of water that should not be used on the garden include toilet waste, the waste from washing machines and dishwashers (as some detergents contain chemicals that are harmful to plants) and also the water from when cleaning a bath if a chemical cleaner was used. Ordinary household soaps – which are used in such small quantity and then are so heavily diluted – will not harm plants. If you are concerned, however, it is not a difficult operation to install a simple replaceable, or washable filter.

Recycling systems have been developed which turns bath, shower and washing-up 'grey' water back to a crystal-clear form that is safe for use. The key to the system is the 'alchemi filter' that effectively removes soaps, detergents and other impurities. The filter sits on top of a standard 55 gallon (210 litre) rainwater butt and a simple diversion takes the grey water from the down-pipe and through the filter into the butt.

Sprin

Tips & tasks

Feeding plants in early spring

Most soft fruits and fruit trees, will flower in mid–spring. If you haven't already done it, early spring is a good time to feed them all. There are three main elements required by plants: nitrogen (N) for good foliage, potassium (K) for successful flower and fruit production, and phosphorous (P) for strong roots. Apply a balanced general fertilizer, such as blood, fish and bone, at about 2½oz per sq yd (70g per sq m). This particular feed releases the

▼ **Give apple trees a feed in early spring, using a balanced fertilizer.**

▲ **Clear greenhouses at the beginning of the season, wiping away any moss or algae.**

nitrogen quickly and phosphate at a slower rate. It can also be used as a soil dressing in advance of planting, and even as a compost 'activator' (something that can help the decomposition process). Other organic fertilizers include dried blood, hoof and horn, bone meal, pelleted poultry manure, seaweed meal and wood ash. The latter is the main organic supply of potash, which is good for counterbalancing any excess of nitrogen in the soil. It can, however, make wet soils stickier, so apply it on a day when the soil is dry, and hoe it into the surface of the soil.

Mulch bush and cane fruits with well–rotted manure or compost to speed growth; keep it away from stems, as it can burn. Ensure soil is moist and weed–free.

Greenhouse plants

Give the greenhouse a tidy up for the new season. Clear away and wash old pots from under the staging. Give the glazing a once–over to wipe away moss or algae that might have accumulated over winter.

Organic tip

Control greenhouse insect pests organically by putting up sticky yellow insect traps.

Scrub the glazing bars with a disinfectant to get rid of any pests or their eggs. And finally, clean out the runs on sliding doors and lubricate them.

You should start increasing the water given to pot plants, as temperatures rise and growth quickens. Foliage plants may benefit from a larger pot.

Apply some shade to the greenhouse before the end of spring to reduce temperatures. Ventilate freely, using the roof vents rather than the side or door vents to avoid draughts. Check plants daily.

Hedges

I HAVE nearly always protected my kitchen gardens over the years by growing a hedge along the perimeter – or at least on the more exposed sides to act as a windbreak. They are also a wonderful haven for wildlife. The trouble is – hedges need trimming, a job I loathe.

Hedges should not be trimmed when frost is likely as the cut surfaces, if frosted, will die back, leaving horrible, brown, dead patches. Late spring would therefore be a more feasible time, when there is little chance of frost damage. There might, however, be a risk of upsetting nesting birds if you do it too early, so maybe early summer is an even better time!

If it gets hot after you've done your trimming, give the whole hedge a quick spray over with the hosepipe (assuming there isn't a hosepipe ban in your area). This will keep the cut surfaces moist, but you might be advised to do it a few times until new shoots appear.

▼ **Only trim hedges at this stage of the season if you are certain there are no nesting birds present.**

Herbs in spring

Buying: Most garden centres stock a range of popular culinary and decorative herbs. Look for healthy, well-established plants. Avoid any that are dried out in their pots or are competing with weeds for survival.

Planting: When you get your plants home, water them and place them in a warm, sheltered site until you are ready to plant them out. Always plant them as soon as possible after purchasing, but avoid planting in hot, dry weather. Dig a hole large enough to hold the plant's roots without cramping them. Remove the plant from its pot, set it in the hole and replace some of the soil around the plant. Firm the soil in, backfill with the rest of the soil and firm it again. Water the plant thoroughly, and then daily in dry weather until it is growing away strongly.

Sowing indoors in early spring: Bergamot, chives, hyssop, lemon verbena, caraway, borage, salad burnet coriander, fenugreek and marjoram.

Sowing outdoors in mid- to late spring: Chervil, hyssop, lemon balm, parsley and dill.

Take cuttings: Catmint, curry plant, lavender, rosemary, sage and thyme.

Divide: Artemesia, rue, chives, comfrey, fennel, hyssop, lovage, salad burnet, sorrel, spearmint, tansy and yarrow.

▲ To divide a clump of chives, lift it and gently split it with your hands into several pieces.

Routine maintenance: It is wise to check evergreens such as bay, hyssop, lavender, rosemary and sage for winter damage to stems. Firm plants in the ground that have been loosened by winter frosts or wind. Prune any new growths lightly to encourage bushy shaped plants and leafy development.

Lawn care in spring

WHETHER you have grass paths dividing up your kitchen garden, or a basic lawn elsewhere, it is likely that the grass will have suffered over the winter and need some attention in spring.

If your lawn contains moss, go over it with a moss killer. There are proprietary chemicals, of course, but the approved organic solution is to water the area with 1 tsp of copper sulphate dissolved in 10 gallons (45 litres) of water. After a day the moss should be dead, so you won't be spreading moss spores everywhere when you scarify the lawn. Do this with a stiff wire-tined rake to 'rough up' the

grass, and really scrape out the dead 'thatch' from underneath. Electric scarifiers are available and they're great for minimizing back-breaking effort.

After you have rid the lawn of thatch, you should spike it. Use a sturdy garden fork to make dozens (or hundreds) of straight holes about 5in (12cm) deep. This lets air into the top layer of soil and helps to relieve compaction. Leave the lawn for another day, and then apply a lawn fertlilizer – dry, sieved or pelletizied chicken manure, or blood and bone. The smell vanishes soon after watering, if the application is not too heavy. Follow this advice and you'll have a superior class of grass this summer.

▼ Spiking the lawn – here with a border fork – allows oxygen down at grass-roots level.

Plant protection

A CLOCHE is invaluable for giving your seeds or young plants a head start. Cloches warm the soil, allowing you to sow or transplant three or four weeks earlier than on open ground. They also protect plants from the wind and hail. And if your soil is prone to 'capping' (developing a hard, compacted surface), a tunnel cloche will help seeds emerge.

The most common cloches (listed in order of heat retention effectiveness) are:

Glass – lets in maximum light and retains the most heat. It is sturdy, fragile and the most expensive. Handled carefully, it will last for years.

Rigid plastic – clear plastic cloches let in maximum light. Double–layered plastic retains heat at night. Durable and lightweight, but bulky to store.

Polythene – cheap, easy to use and compact to store. Wire hoops are needed to support the sheets. Retains the least heat at night and condensation can be a problem.

Fleece – for the protection of delicate young seedlings and transplants. Doesn't retain much heat, but protects against frost. It allows water and air in.

Mesh/Netting – provides some shade rather than raising soil temperatures. Useful barrier against pests such as carrot root fly and cabbage white butterfly.

If you are already growing early blossoming fruit trees and bushes – such as peaches, nectarines or apricots – you may need to protect them from frost. Frost can damage the fragile flowers and prevent fruit from forming. If you site your plants away from frost pockets (cold, low–lying areas or against east–facing walls), then you are less likely to suffer problems, but it's still best to be cautious.

If you live in an area where frost is likely to persist, you may wish to erect a semi–permanent barrier of glass or plastic – but make sure you allow access to insects for pollination. If it's only a cold night here or there, you can wrap your small bushes and trees with fleece or use a plant cosie. Remove once danger of frost has passed.

Organic tip

If you have a close-mesh fruit cage, open one side of it to allow pollinating insects to visit blooms. However, keep an eye out for birds that are partial to fruit buds.

Pollination

M OST gardeners do seem to think that fruit trees need attention only when it's close to the time for picking, or at least well after the formation of the fruits themselves.

The truth is that without flowers there will be no fruits, and flowers of fruiting plants usually appear in the spring. So this is an extremely important time to pay the trees some attention – especially in the form of protecting the blossom.

With large freestanding trees this is not particularly practicable, but it certainly is with trained trees (fan, espalier or cordon). It is particularly

◀ **Individual fruiting plants, such as currants, can be enveloped in fleece if a frost is forecast.**

▲ **Rigid polythene cloches let in maximum light and reasonable heat is retained at night.**

important for apricots, peaches and nectarines not to be frosted when the blossom is out. Cover the plants with horticultural fleece or sacking.

The problem then, of course, is that you will be preventing pollinating insects, ie bees, from gaining access to the blooms, so they won't be able to do their important work. To facilitate pollination you'll need to do it by hand. Here's how...

In the middle of the day during a warm and dry spell, gently (very gently) transfer the pollen from the flower anthers to the stigmas by using a soft brush, or a piece of cotton wool on a matchstick.

If you are unsure which bits of a flower are which, just dab the brush or cotton wool on all parts of the centre of the flower, and move from blossom to blossom doing the same thing. But I can't emphasize enough that you need to do it gently! You should do this frequently too, until flowering is finished.

Propagation

DEPENDING on your vegetable preferences, it's a toss-up between early and late spring as being the busiest times to sow many types of seed. In early spring the hardier types and early salad veg are sown. In late spring, you can still sow these, as well as others.

As your vegetable seeds germinate in spring they will need pricking out. Always try to prick out seedlings at the point at which the seed leaves have formed. Handle them with care and avoid touching the stem. Loosen the soil around a seedling with a dibber before gently pulling on the leaves.

If you are pricking out lots of seedlings, it's perhaps best to knock them out of the pot or tray, ensuring that no damage is caused to the root system. But if you do this, don't waste any time, as you will have exposed many of the fine roots to the drying effects of the air.

The potting compost should be good quality and peat-free, and it should state on the bag that it is suitable for young seedlings. Make a small hole for the seedling, lower it in and firm it in gently. Only the leaves should be exposed above the compost.

Water the seedlings in with tapwater – rainwater contains a surprising amount of bacteria and other impurities that, in

▲ **Vegetable seedlings should be kept in an unheated greenhouse until it is warm enough outside.**

normal, day-to-day gardening, does not matter. Seedlings, though, are more fragile and susceptible, and tapwater is better for them at this stage.

Use a watering can with a fine rose, so that the spray doesn't wash them out of the compost.

Reduce the risk of 'damping off' (a fungal disease affecting seedlings) by only watering sparingly until the seedlings have produced a good root system. Ventilate the area daily, as temperatures in unventilated greenhouses can soar rapidly.

Harden off seedlings when they are big enough – this means slowly acclimatizing them to outside conditions.

◄ **Use a watering can with a fine rose when watering seedling plants.**

▲ **Liming a soil can 'sweeten' it by reducing its level of acidity – but do this sparingly.**

Soil preparation

Prepare light soils for sowing and planting by digging and forking, and then incorporate some well–rotted organic matter where required.

Use a kit to test your soil for lime and nutrient content. This is particularly important on new plots where you don't already know the level of nutrition in the ground. If your soil is a bit acidic, you may well need to add some lime to it.

Lime is a word that is often used so loosely that it no longer has any definite meaning. There are two main types of liming material commonly available: ground limestone, also called ground chalk or carbonate of lime – $CaCO_3$; hydrated lime, also known as slaked lime or calcium hydroxide – $Ca(OH)_2$. Quicklime, also referred to as burnt lime, or calcium oxide – CaO, may also be found but this is not so common; if you have this, apply it at roughly half the rate of ground limestone.

How to reduce soil acidity*

	Addition of ground limestone	Addition of hydrated lime
Sandy soil	6oz per sq yd (203g per m²)	5oz per sq yd (170g per m²)
Loam soil	9oz per sq yd (306g per m²)	7oz per sq yd (240g per m²)
Clay Soil	13oz per sq yd (443g per m²)	9oz per sq yd (306g per m²)

*The quantities given are sufficient to reduce soil acidity by one pH unit. This is the scale by which acidity and alkalinity is measured (via the concentration of hydrogen ions in water, expressed as 'pH', or 'percentage hydrogen'). The scale is divided from 0 to 14, including decimal placings. The 'neutral' point is pH 7.0. Figures below pH 7.0 indicate acidic conditions; the lower the figure the more acidic the soil. Figures above pH 7.0 indicate alkalinity; the higher the figure the stronger the degree of alkalinity. A change of just one pH unit represents a change of x10 in acidity/alkalinity; a change of 2 pH units therefore represents a change of x100 in acidity/alkalinity, and so on. Thus the alkalinity at pH 10.0 is one thousand times the alkalinity at pH 7.0.

The following is a list of specific pH levels that may help in understanding the relevance:

pH 13.9	Caustic soda
pH 12.4	Lime water
pH 12.0	Bleach
pH 11.0	Ammonia
pH 9.0	Antacid tablets
pH 8.5	Upper limit on chalky soil
pH 8.0	Sea water/baking soda
pH 7.0	Neutral point (also pure water, human blood and cow's milk)
pH 6.5	**The ideal pH for soil (the level which suits the vast majority of plants)**
pH 5.7	Saturated carbonic acid (strong acid rain)
pH 4.0 (approx)	The lower limit for most soils (also beer/coffee)
pH 3.0	Vinegar
pH 2.6	Strong lemon juice
pH 0.5	Battery acid
pH 0.1	Hydrochloric acid

Supporting plants

WITH all plants growing with relative speed in spring, staking the floppy ones should be on your list of things to do. The classic stakes are, of course, bamboo canes, ideal for staking tall, single stems.

Flexible canes also make good stakes if you poke both ends into the soil and create a low arch in the middle to hold back plants.

Pea sticks look great if you're trying to achieve an informal look. Birch and hazel work best as they're bendy and twiggy, but of course you need a ready supply, and to collect them before they leaf up. They're ideal for the vegetable garden.

Ring-type stakes work quite well for clump forming plants. Use some plastic-coated, wire-linked stakes for really floppy plants. Use them in a triangular shape for strength, and if you have a large clump to stake, use two or three triangles.

Watering

AWAY to minimize drought risk to plants is to make use of some water-absorbing gel crystals (which can be bought from garden centres) in your containers. Add them now when potting and planting.

Weeds, pests and diseases

SLUGS always bring out the worst in me. They sneakily attack seedlings and bedding plants in the dead of night, and I take their chomping very personally. But I'm never going back to nasty, poisonous pellets. I've tried various alternatives, with mixed results: there are one or two plants in pots that I'm determined should not be attacked, so I shall scatter a few handfuls of crushed eggshells around the bases.

▼ **Birch twigs used to support plants may appear obtrusive, but they soon become concealed.**

▲ **Crushed eggshells scattered around susceptible plants is a good way to deter slugs and snails.**

Keep looking out for any pests attacking pot–grown fruits, such as gooseberries, currants and apples. Caterpillars should be picked off; scale insects should be scraped or rubbed off.

Fork gently around the base of soft and cane fruits to help expose pests, including chafer grubs and vine weevils, to the hungry bird population.

Common garden weeds

W EEDING is never more important than in spring. Keep the hoe going to keep the annual weeds under control.

Bindweed Perennial; thin but deep and persistent roots work their way between the roots of cultivated border plants; shoots twine around and climb up border plants; clear by mulching with carpet or black plastic for at least a whole season.

▲ **It is best to hoe out chickweed, preferably when it is small, as it breaks easily when pulled.**

Chickweed Annual; seeds itself prolifically and grows all year round; it easily hoes, but do not pull by hand as it breaks easily; clear a seedbed before sowing and hoe as soon as seen.

Creeping buttercup Perennial; stems creep along just above ground level; more of a lawn problem; can be controlled by mulching, and can be hoed out of a border or kitchen garden situation.

Couch grass Perennial; white rhizomes sprout underground at intervals to form new clumps; control by long–term mulching, continually turning over the soil with a rotary cultivator and removing all traces of weeds, and/or double digging.

Dandelion Perennial; a single deep taproot that sprouts again if broken; fork out the entire roots, and don't let the plants produce or disperse the seed.

Dock Perennial; control as for dandelion.

Ground elder Perennial; clumps form from shallow roots; control as for couch grass.

Groundsel Annual; grows all year round; easy to pull by hand or hoe out.

Hairy bittercress Annual; pods explode dispersing seed over a wide area; control by hand–weeding, hoeing and watching that they don't flower.

Horsetail Perennial; deep and penetrating black rhizomatous roots that can easily snap and re-grow; control in the same way as bindweed.

Meadow grass Annual; clumps of grass with shallow, fibrous roots; grows all year round; not easy to hoe, so mulching is the best control.

Nettle Annual and perennial forms; hoe annual forms; dig out perennial forms or use a long–term mulch, and continually cutting them wears them out fairly easily.

▼ **Groundsel, a member of the daisy family, is an annual weed and is easily pulled by hand.**

Fruit

Apples

 You may still have one or two apples in store from the autumn. Use them up now, otherwise they'll be past being good.

 If your apple trees suffer regular bouts of fungal diseases, such as mildew and scab, give them a regular, fortnightly spray until mid-summer with an organic copper-based fungicide such as Bordeaux Mixture.

 Nip off blooms from newly planted apples to allow them to form a stocky framework before they start fruiting.

▼ **Use up your last remaining stored apples before they go off.**

Blackcurrants

 Check blackcurrant bushes for gall mites that can attack the buds, making them swell. Remove any infected buds and burn them.

 Feed blackcurrants in early spring with a fertilizer that is high in nitrogen, such as dried blood. It will give them a good start.

 If you're planting any new bushes, cut them back at planting time to within two buds of the base and spray with any insecticide approved by the Soil Association for the control of aphids, capsids and caterpillars.

Small garden tip

Even if all you have is a balcony or a bit of a terrace, you can still grow apples. You'll just have to go for something like a 'Ballerina' or 'Minarette' apple tree. Both types grow on a single vertical trunk and no pruning is necessary. The yield is good, considering the small space they take up.

 For a good crop of gooseberries in early summer, prune, weed and feed them in spring.

Gooseberries

 Gooseberries can be pruned in early spring as the sap is beginning to rise – it means wounds will heal faster. This lessens the risk of infection from grey mould and coral spot, to which they are prone. Pruning now also allows you to remove any winter damage. Cut side shoots back to two buds from the base. If the bush is fairly new – up to three or four years old – the leader (the central leading shoot) should be cut back by about a third. If the bush is mature, the height will already be quite established.

In late spring you will start to see the tiny berries beginning to swell. If the crop appears to be heavy, thin it at this time. Remove some of the berries when they are large enough to use in cooking – and do this in stages until the fruits that are left to mature are about 2in (5cm) apart.

 In early spring, weed carefully around your plants. Sprinkle some fish, blood and bone fertilizer, an organically based mixture, around the plants at a loose handful to ten square foot (one square metre) of soil.

 Gooseberries mainly flower during late spring, and you should still make sure that they are protected from any sudden frosts, otherwise you could lose all of the year's fruiting potential. It is a good idea to cover the plants at night with fleece, netting or sacking if frosts still threaten to strike.

The gooseberry sawfly is a common pest that may be evident in late spring on your plants. Look out for the larvae between late spring and mid-summer. The full-sized larvae are about ¾in (2cm) long, with black heads and pale green bodies with black spots. They eat the leaves (but not the fruit), with the result that the plants lose vigour in subsequent years. The pests can also attack red and white currants. Regularly inspect the plants, especially the more protected parts of the plant in the centre, removing any larvae you see by hand.

Weeding around the plants can also be important in late spring. But don't hoe between the plants as this can damage the surface roots and lead to suckering, which is a waste of the plants' energy, and a nuisance for you to pull out. It is far better to weed by hand.

Melons

 Early spring is a good time to sow seed of melons and there are some great varieties available. I normally grow 'Ogen', which reliably produces plenty of tasty fruits. Other good varieties include the salmon–pink flesh of 'Charentais', the orange–striped 'Tigger' and 'Minnesota Midget' – which claims to be one of the sweetest and which I can recommend.

▲ **Sow the seed of outdoor melons in mid-spring.**

Sow seed in early spring for indoor greenhouse crops, or delay until mid–spring if you're going to grow them outside. Sow in a 3in (7.5cm) pot of peat–free seed compost, one seed per pot. Water in and place in a well–lit spot at roughly 20°C – a heated propagator is ideal.

 Grow the seedlings on at 18°C and, when their roots fill the pot, plant singly into a 12in (30cm) diameter pot, or three in a standard growbag. In late spring, harden off any young plants to be grown outside. Erect a string or wire support for each plant and begin feeding with tomato fertilizer. Cropping could start by mid–summer, lasting until early autumn.

Pears

In early spring, use up any stored pears from the previous autumn while they are still good to eat.

If pear trees have any fungal diseases, like mildew and scab, give them a fortnightly spray until mid–summer with an organic copper–based fungicide such as Bordeaux Mixture.

Nip off blooms from newly planted pears to help form a stocky fruiting framework.

▶ **Pears stored in the autumn should now be eaten as they will soon start to deteriorate.**

 Pepinos produce very attractive oval fruits that start off a pale green, then develop lovely purple stripes as they ripen.

vitamin C and have a sweet flavour similar to a combination of melon and pear.

Raspberries

 In mid–spring, fasten your summer–fruiting raspberry canes well, to prevent wind–rock.

 In late spring, pull up raspberry shoots that cause overcrowding, or those growing too far out to be able to tie in.

 Raspberries may still be planted up until mid–spring, when the soil and weather conditions are favourable. In fact, they could have been planted at any time since late autumn. Space canes 15–18in (38–45cm) apart in the rows, and cut them back to 12in (30cm) directly after planting. The top roots of the canes should be about 2in (5cm) below the soil surface. Allow 5–6ft (1.5–1.8m) between rows.

Pepino

THIS relatively new annual summer–flowering plant appears on the market under the brand name of Pepino. Its botanical name is *Solanum muricatum* 'Aiton', and it was discovered as a seedling in Peru and Columbia and is very noticeable for its colourful clusters of flowers and fruit. Pepino can grow up to 3ft (90cm) high and not quite so wide. It is attractive as a patio or terrace container plant. Its soft, green, elongated leaves are 15cm (6in) long and contrast beautifully with the flowers and the fruit. During its flowering season, from late spring to early autumn, it produces clusters of lovely purple and white striped flowers. It bears its first fruit as soon as early summer.

The fruit is oval and can grow to 5in (12cm) long with a diameter of 3in (7.5cm). Initially it is pale green but as it ripens it develops purple stripes and streaks like the flowers. The fruit ripens best in the full sun and on the plant, where its colour gradually changes to purple and yellow. The first fruits are ready to be eaten from mid–summer, and they contain plenty of juice and

Rhubarb

FORCE rhubarb for an early crop (see page 150). Cover the dormant buds with straw or dry leaves inside a forcing pot or large bucket that excludes light. Tender pink stems will emerge in a few weeks' time.

 You should divide rhubarb every four or five years – if yours is producing fewer and shorter stalks, it needs splitting. Mid–spring, as the soil is warming up, is the best time to do this. Lift up the plant completely and then remove all bits of root from the soil. Fork over the area and then add some well–rotted compost. Add a few handfuls of blood and bone fertilizer.

The old plant may be cut up into probably four or five 'sets', each of which should have at least one bud. These can then be replanted, 3ft (90cm) apart, with the buds just below the surface.

▼ **Rhubarb makes a fine plant for growing in a patio container – as long as the container is large.**

Resulting 'sets' can also be potted up in a tub for growing on the patio and, as long as the container is sizeable, the plant is watered and fed well, the rhubarb should make a good container crop. Don't fill the pot with soil or growing compost to the rim, instead stop when it is three–quarters full. Plant the rhubarb firmly and water it in. Then place a mulch of well–rotted compost or manure on the surface, but not actually touching the rhubarb plant. This mulch will slowly be taken down into the soil around the roots, and it will also help to prevent weed growth in the container. You should not pick any stems in the first year; wait until next year, after the plant has established itself and has some good, healthy roots.

 Rhubarb can start to be harvested from mid–spring. Hold the stalk close to the ground and pull upwards with a twisting motion. Do not strip the plant – always leave four stalks or more, to allow the plant to continue growing. Don't pull any stalks after mid–summer, to give the plant a good, long rest.

Stone fruits

DRUPE is the name given to fruiting plants that produce a stone, or the large, hard seed in the middle of the fleshy fruit. These include peaches, nectarines and apricots. If you have any of these (as well as almonds) growing in trained form against a sunny wall, mid–spring is the time to remove the covers that have protected them through the winter from frost and peach leaf curl disease.

 Newly planted stone fruits, such as cherries, peaches, nectarines, apricots and almonds, should be pruned during mid–spring. You should not prune established plants as doing it now could

encourage bacterial canker and a disease called silver leaf. But healthy, newly planted fruits need to get roots established and pruning each side or lateral shoot back by half will help to achieve this. Remove those shoots growing backwards into the wall or fence. And stop those growing directly outwards, after a couple of leaves from the base. Leave the shoots that are extending sideways – unless they have reached the limits of the space available to them. Tie in well all the shoots that need to be secured.

Thin the fruits of established plants now. If you allow too many fruits to develop, this will weaken the plant and it will produce many, much smaller fruits. Thin nectarine fruits to about 6in (15cm) apart, and the other fruits to 8–10in (20–25cm) apart to encourage fewer but larger fruits. Do this when the fruits are the size of marbles.

Strawberries

Y OU can buy either potted strawberry plants, or freshly dug runners in early spring. It is better to buy from a specialist nursery, as they will have a good choice of varieties, grown to exacting health standards.

Strawberries like to be in a sunny, sheltered, weed–free spot in soil with plenty of organic matter added. They dislike waterlogged soils. Scatter about a handful of general–purpose fertilizer over the bed before planting. Set the plants 24–30in (60–75cm) apart.

▲ **Plant strawberries in a weed-free, sunny and sheltered position.**

If space allows, a block of three short rows makes for a neater strawberry bed. The planting depth is crucial – not too deep and not too high. Also, make sure the plants are firmed in well afterwards.

Protect your flowering strawberries in pots from the attentions of slugs and snails. Put down beer traps or use biological nematode controls. Using these controls little and often is the key.

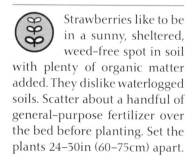

Organic tip

If you can be patient enough for fruit, planting a bed of strawberries and nipping out all the flowers as they appear in the first year, will build up the plants for next year.

Small garden tip

Sow the seeds of alpine strawberries throughout spring: these little plants are perfect for planting in pots and window-boxes and in a small garden as edging for a low bed. As an added bonus, these mini strawberries also have a superb flavour.

In early spring, shield strawberries from icy winds by covering them with cloches; seal both ends of the cloches to avoid creating a wind tunnel. When flowers appear, move alternate cloches away, so that bees and pollinating insects have access. Protect flowering strawberries from night frosts by covering the plants with fleece, or you could even try newspaper.

Some of the fruits of greenhouse-grown strawberries will be ready for picking in early spring (depending on sunlight levels). Greenhouse strawberries are great, as they are the first of the homegrown fruits of the year, and for this reason they seem to taste all the better for it.

Vegetables

◀ **Asparagus spears should be cut when they are 6–8in (15–20cm) long.**

Asparagus

 Asparagus can be cut over a six- to eight-week period, and late spring is the key time for cutting. But don't cut if your plants are two years old or younger, as you will be weakening them; they won't have had enough time in the ground to build up an established root system. Cut when the spears are 6–8in (15–20cm) tall. Use a sharp knife, and make the cut some 2–4in (5–10cm) below soil level. Cut frequently, as the spears should not be allowed to grow too high. New spears will emerge shortly.

Keep harvesting for six weeks, cutting every day if necessary. But at the end of this period you should leave the plants alone. The spears should be allowed to grow into ferns, in order to build up reserves for next year's crop. Asparagus is best when eaten immediately but will keep for up to two weeks in the fridge (do not wash before storing, as the moisture can induce rotting).

 The main pest to affect this vegetable is the asparagus beetle. It is actually the grub of the beetle that does the damage, and can completely defoliate the fern if left unchecked. This will reduce the plant's ability to feed the crowns for the following season. Pick off the black and yellow adult beetles as you see them.

Aubergines

AUBERGINES (or 'eggplants') are semi-tropical plants, but in most seasons will crop successfully in the greenhouse, and will succeed in exceptional summers outside in full sun.

 I tend to keep all my aubergine growing to inside the greenhouse, by sowing the seed in mid- to late winter in the required temperature of 61°F (16°C). In early spring the seedlings can be pricked out first into 3in (7.5cm) pots, and then five or six weeks later into 7in (18cm) pots, using a light, open peat-free compost.

Whether kept to fruit under glass or planted outside, it is important to feed aubergines regularly. A thinly diluted feed of seaweed solution could be made with every watering. In hot weather, this could be every day.

▶ **Beetroot can be sown directly outdoors from early spring until late summer.**

Beetroot

 Sow seeds of beetroot in early spring. Sow in drills 1in (2.5cm) deep and 12in (30cm) apart. The seed should be sown two together, with 4in (10cm) between each pair of seeds. When the young seedlings are about 1in (2.5cm) high, thin them out to leave a single plant at each station.

Broad beans

 Sow broad beans in the open from early to mid–spring, if the soil and weather conditions permit.

 Keep an eye open for problem blackfly on broad beans. Control them on fully grown plants by

pinching out and destroying the tips, where most of the aphids tend to gather.

▼ **Broad bean flowers can be attractive in their own right – but they don't last long.**

Cabbage (spring)

 Spring cabbage should be coming to maturity and be ready to pick in early to mid–spring.

▼ **Spring cabbages are ready for cutting during spring, but watch out for damage from wood pigeons.**

Cabbage (summer)

 Summer cabbage can be harvested from the early summer until autumn. For the earliest crops, sowing should take place in early spring. You'll need to choose an early variety:

'Greyhound' an old favourite – the compact, pointed heads mature quickly. A good choice for early sowing.

'Hispi' a modern variety, one of the quickest to mature.

'Primo (Golden Acre)' the most popular ball–headed summer cabbage; compact and firm.

'Stonehead' an F1 hybrid which produces heavy round heads; stands well without splitting.

'Winnigstadt' the large, pointed heads of this old favourite are ready for cutting in early to mid–autumn.

Sow seed thinly in 1in (2.5cm) deep drills, 6in (15cm) apart. Water the drills beforehand to encourage speedy germination, and cover the row with cloches.

 Transplant seedlings when they are about 6in (15cm) tall, at any time during spring. The young plants will need firming in well, and to be given plenty of water.

Carrots

 Late spring is the key time for sowing your carrots. The seedlings will come up a week or so after sowing, and when they're large enough to be handled, thin them to about 1in (2.5cm) apart.

After a month or so thin them again to 2in (5cm), using the baby carrots you thin out for salads and cooking.

 There is no worse a pest to carrots than carrot fly. The fact that there are no chemical products that are currently licensed to kill it has no bearing on us – as we wouldn't be using them anyway! Dispose of thinnings away from the bed, as the smell will attract the fly. To confuse it, so it flies over the top of the crop without venturing down to lay its eggs, either cover the crop

Organic tip

Grow onions or leeks next to carrots – their smell helps to repel carrot root fly. Salsify is another root crop that, it is said, will repel the fly and so too will strong-smelling, woody herbs such as rosemary, sage and wormwood.

with some horticultural fleece throughout the season, or build a 'wall' of polythene or wood around the crop at least 2ft (60cm) high.

▼ **Organic carrots can be enjoyed throughout the summer, but they'll need to be sown in spring.**

Cauliflowers

I LOVE cauliflower; in fact, all brassicas, but cauliflower is one of my favourites. With a delicate cheese sauce you have a meal on its own.

 Sow seeds of some of the summer–maturing varieties during spring outside. The drills should be ½in (1cm) deep and 6in (15cm) apart. Sow the seed thinly and cover with soil. Thin the seedlings to prevent them from becoming weak and spindly; ideally to around 3in (7.5cm) apart.

 When the plants have five or six leaves they will then be ready for transplanting into their final growing positions. For picking details, see pages 83 and 154.

 In spring, harvest your winter cauliflowers. Cut them at the base of the stem with a sharp knife before the curd opens up.

Celeriac

 Continue to harvest celeriac in the early part of spring.

 Sowing takes place in mid–spring (usually in a greenhouse) and the plants are planted outdoors in early summer.

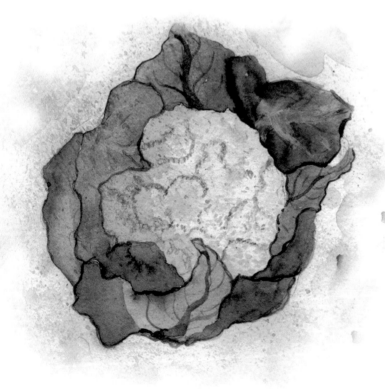

Celery

I THINK the traditional trench–grown celery varieties are much better than any of the modern self–blanching types. If you only have limited space available to grow it, bear in mind that it needs 15in (37cm) between rows and 9in (23cm) between plants in the rows.

 Seed can be sown in early to mid–spring, needing some heat and a greenhouse.

Prepare trenches for your celery in mid–spring; they will not be wanted until early summer, but if you prepare well in advance, the manure and soil will become blended together.

Chillis

See Peppers

Courgettes & Marrows

Sow the large, flat seeds of courgettes (sometimes known as 'zucchini') and marrows in mid–spring in 3in (7.5cm) pots, or large modules. Alternatively, sow two or three seeds in situ under jam jars in late spring and thin out the weakest seedlings to leave one per plant. Sow the seeds on their edge rather than upright, as this reduces the soil resistance for the tiny emerging seedlings.

Cucumbers

INDOOR cucumbers, that are grown in a greenhouse can also be known as 'frame' cucumbers. They need warmth and regular attention – watering, feeding, tying and stopping. They can be a challenge! The oldest variety, and for me perhaps the best, is 'Telegraph' (named when the telegraph was a new invention, and because the fruit is long and straight, like a telegraph pole).

 May is the ideal month to sow them in a warm greenhouse. Place one or two seeds into a 3in (7.5cm) pot; sow the seed edgeways (vertically) as this reduces soil resistance for the emerging seedlings. Use a normal seed compost, and set the seed just under the surface.

 Plant the young plants into growing bags, or a greenhouse border, after about a month. Outdoor cucumbers are known as 'ridge' cucumbers. Sow them under glass and plant them outside after all risk of frost has passed.

▼ **'Telegraph' is one of the oldest varieties of greenhouse or 'frame' cucumber.**

Endives

 During spring endives will be starting to reach maturity and be ready for picking.

French beans

DWARF French beans mature earlier than the climbing French beans, but the yield is usually heavier on climbers.

 Sow the seeds under cover in mid- to late spring. This can be in pots or modules, or outdoors under cloches – because French beans are sensitive to frost and need at least 54°F (12°C) to germinate. Plant out when the seedlings are about 3in (7.5cm).

Alternatively you can sow them direct into the garden soil, having first put the supports in place, and keeping a close eye on the weather forecasts, as the risk of frost may still be there up until late spring.

For a continuous crop of beans into autumn, sow direct into moist soil every two weeks until mid–summer. They should be ready for picking in eight to ten weeks from sowing.

Garlic

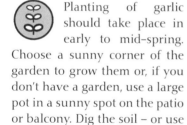

Planting of garlic should take place in early to mid-spring. Choose a sunny corner of the garden to grow them or, if you don't have a garden, use a large pot in a sunny spot on the patio or balcony. Dig the soil – or use peat–free potting compost – and sprinkle a handful of organic general fertilizer, like seaweed or blood, fish and bone.

Take a bulb and split it into its clove sections, planting these just under the surface of the soil about 6in (15cm) apart. Apart

▲ **For a continuous crop of French beans, sow seeds every two weeks from mid-spring to mid-summer.**

from watering in dry weather, there is nothing else to do until the foliage turns yellow, during late summer.

▼ **Garlic is from the Mediterranean region, yet it can withstand quite cold winter temperatures.**

Jerusalem artichokes

THESE are tall plants with edible tubers. When cooked they have a distinct chestnut–like flavour and texture. The above–ground parts can reach 10ft (3m) or more, so you will need to give this plant some space in which to grow. They are not fussy plants, and although they are undoubtedly at their best in full sun, they will tolerate and perform well in dappled light and half shade.

The tubers should be planted in early spring, but in the previous winter you should have dug in some well–rotted compost. Without this treatment the resultant tubers are likely to be fewer and smaller. Set the tubers 3in (7.5cm) deep and about 18in (45cm) apart. 'Fuseau' has a smoothish skin; 'Boston Red' has a rose–red skin and is a particularly knobbly variety. For lifting, see page 121.

Kale

 Kale will be reaching maturity and be ready for harvesting.

Leeks

 Sow outdoors in drills in late spring. Thin seedlings out.

 Leeks that were sown in early summer and transplanted in mid–summer will be reaching their maturity during spring and can be harvested.

Organic tip

Leeks need an open site and a rich soil. Dig in well-rotted compost or manure in the winter before planting. If you want to grow large leeks, a long growing season is required. However, a good yield of smaller leeks can be obtained by closer planting. Keep leeks well weeded, and when the plants are established mulch them with some well-rotted compost, if it is available.

Lettuce

 Sow seed very thinly, ¼in (6mm) deep or so, in a mix of garden soil and peat–free compost. The seedlings will germinate within a week or so and as soon as they are big enough to handle, you should prick them out into larger pots for planting out.

 Plant out at about 12in (30cm) apart. Lettuce that was sown back in autumn can be planted out under cloches in early spring, or in a cold frame, to provide some useful lettuce crops from mid–spring onwards.

Small garden tip

Lettuce is a perfect container plant and can be grown successfully in everything from pots or growing bags to window–boxes. It will even grow well if the area is lightly shaded.

▼ **Lettuce 'Little Gem' is a quick-maturing semi-cos lettuce with delicious, crisp leaves.**

Slugs can be a problem with lettuce, so choose your preferred control method (beer 'pubs' work well, but the biological nematode controls are almost certainly more effective).

 Always water lettuce plants in the morning as watering them in the cooler evening increases the chance of disease.

Marrows

See Courgettes

New Zealand spinach

THIS crop makes a tasty alternative to the normal kind of spinach, which has a tendency to bolt. It has spiky, triangular leaves and can reach 24in (60cm) high and has a trailing habit, which makes it a useful and ornamental ground cover plant, as well as a good container plant. It can survive on much less water than similar vegetables and, as long as the soil has good organic content, it does not require additional fertilizer – great for organic gardeners!

 Successive sowings can be made of New Zealand spinach in a greenhouse, or in a cold frame in mid-spring. Sow the seed singly in 20in (8cm) pots, pre-soaking in water for 24 hours to assist germination. Place the pots in a cool greenhouse or cold frame.

 When they are big enough to handle – between two and four weeks – the seedlings will need transplanting. They can then be planted out once all risk of frost has passed.

Onions & Shallots

MANY gardeners think of shallots as being a distinct type of vegetable in their own right, but in fact they are simply a species of onion. These are available as small bulbs, for planting in mid- to late winter, and for harvesting in mid-summer. They are milder in flavour than onions. There is not a great deal of work attached to growing them, particularly in spring, other than to keep them weed-free and to water them only if the weather is hot and dry for a prolonged period of time. For planting, see page 123; for harvesting, see page 89.

◀ **It is important to feed onions with a general organic fertilizer in spring if you want the bulbs to grow large.**

Small garden tip

Spring onions don't need a lot of space in which to grow. Because of their size and habit of growth they are very suited to containers. Make your sowings throughout the spring, picking after six to eight weeks.

Some favourite onion varieties of mine are 'Brunswick' and 'Bedfordshire Champion'. The first is a mild-tasting bulb onion with blood-red outer skin, and the latter is a globe onion with a strong taste.

 Sow seed in open ground in early spring, in rows 12in (30cm) apart. Thin the seedlings before they start encroaching on each other's space.

During early spring, sprinkle some general organic fertilizer, such as fish, blood and bone meal onto the soil around Japanese onions sown last summer.

Onions (spring)

THE one vegetable I grow year in year out is the versatile spring onion, or salad onion. Also known as bunching onions, they are really quick and easy to grow. The oldest and best-known variety is 'White Lisbon', with a silvery skin and a mild flavour. 'Guardsman' can stand a long time in the ground without bulbing up (overgrowing) and becoming too dry and strong in flavour.

 For the highest yield, sow thinly in rows 4–6in (10–15cm) apart so no thinning is required. Just cover the seeds with soil, and water in dry spells.

Sow from early to mid-spring and you'll have a crop from late spring until the end of summer.

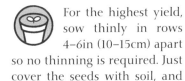

Parsnips

 Sow parsnip seed in cultivated soil that has a fine tilth.

Peas

NOTHING tastes better than peas straight from the pod. But if you want to be sure of a good crop, you need to get sowing sooner rather than later. By setting them off as early as possible in spring you ensure the strongest, healthiest root system. This makes them more drought-resistant later in the year and will help ensure high yields. 'Onwards' is a tasty, reliable variety, or if you want a dwarf try 'Little Marvel'.

Peas don't like a cold spring soil, so I start them off in 3in (7.5cm) square pots, sowing two seeds

▲ **Fresh peas straight from the pod are a wonderful treat. Sow them as early as possible in spring.**

in opposite corners at a depth of 1in (2.5cm). They're easily separated when it comes to transplanting in mid-spring. Germinate on a cool windowsill or in a frost-free greenhouse.

▼ **Wide, flat-bottomed drills are the traditional way to sow peas.**

Peas can still be sown later in spring directly in the ground. Make a drill in the kitchen garden soil, about 5cm (2in) deep. Traditionally, wide drills were created, with flat bottoms, and the peas were 'sprinkled' or 'broadcast sown' into the drill. This way they grew up to support themselves – with the help of posts and wire.

Lots of peas will grow up in close proximity, but because you don't need to walk between them to harvest them, it makes good use of space. Cover the rows with wire netting to keep marauding birds away.

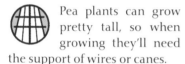 Pea plants can grow pretty tall, so when growing they'll need the support of wires or canes.

Peppers & Chillis

 Sow seeds in early spring. It's a good idea to sow two seeds per 3in (7.5cm) pot and to remove the weakest seedling. The seeds germinate in a temperature of 50–70°F (15–20°C).

 Pepper and chilli seeds that were sown in the greenhouse in early spring should be ready for final planting or potting on by mid- to late spring. If you did not manage to get any sowing done, garden centres frequently have young pepper plants for sale, but you will be limited as to the

▼ **Peppers, or members of the Capsicum family, look perfectly at home in the flower garden too.**

varieties on offer. Plant two or three plants to each growing bag, or one plant per 8–10in (20–25cm) pot, using growing bag compost.

 Feed the plants with a liquid fertilizer – such as seaweed – once a week, and also maintain high humidity by damping down twice a day in hot weather if possible. Larger or high-yielding plants may need staking during early summer.

Mist the plants regularly to keep down red spider mite and encourage the fruits to set. Water the plants regularly as it is not a good idea to let the compost dry out – but equally, it should not be sodden either. Pinching out the growing tip of these plants is not recommended.

Small garden tip

To save space, you can use thick black bin liners to grow potatoes in. Put some compost and soil in the bottom of a bag, then space out half a dozen seed potato tubers, and cover them with more soil. As the green growths appear, roll up more of the liner and add more soil until you get to the top of the bag. I've also seen gardeners plant spuds in soil in the centre of two tyres laid flat and stacked. When the top growth appears, stack another tyre on top and fill with soil. You can do this a few more times as well, to create a tower five or six deep.

Potatoes

 Seed potatoes will be on sale in early spring, and they should be 'chitted' (meaning the eyes have sprouted into 1in (2.5cm) long shoots) for six weeks before planting. This is important with early varieties, which have a short growing period, and is useful for maincrops in colder areas where planting should take place later. Tubers that have been chitted will grow away quickly once planted.

Place a single layer of tubers in a box with just enough dry compost in the bottom to hold them upright. The 'rose' end – where most of the eyes are – should point upwards. Keep the box in a frost-free airy place, out of the sun. In six weeks, the tubers will be sturdy, with a number of short sprouts, and ready for planting. Don't remove any sprouts – the number is not a significant factor, but the length of each one is. The longer the sprout, the greater the chance it will snap off or fail once planted.

 Once the seed potatoes have been chitted they should be planted out. They prefer to grow in a site that is open, fertile and preferably slightly acidic in nature. Set each tuber in a drill or hole some 5in (12cm) deep. Early varieties should be around 12in (30cm) apart in rows 24in (60cm) apart, and maincrop varieties should be 15in (37.5cm) apart in rows 30in (75cm) apart.

Carefully replace the soil over the tubers, and using a rake make a slight ridge of soil over the row. Potato plants need much volume of soil in which to develop their underground stems and tubers, so making a ridge, and later 'earthing up', helps to create this volume.

 Mound the soil over emerging shoots of potatoes to protect them from late frosts. This also encourages more potatoes to form and makes them easier to lift when it's harvest time.

▼ **Chitted potato tubers (or 'seed' as they are known) should be planted 12in (30cm) apart.**

 Spring-sown pumpkins, such as this, need a good, warm summer to help them swell.

Pumpkins & Squashes

PUMPKINS and squashes can all be sown in mid–spring for planting out in early summer. Pumpkin seeds sown at this time will be ready for harvesting in time for Halloween.

Sow the large, flat seeds in 3in (7.5cm) pots, or large modules. It's a good idea to sow the seeds on edge rather than upright, as this reduces soil resistance for the emerging seedlings.

Radishes

Sow radish seed in cultivated soil that has a fine tilth. Summer pulling varieties can be white or red, round or cylindrical (the winter–pulling radishes are black and usually round or long–rooted).

Radishes are quick–to–mature plants, so any sown about two months previously will be reaching maturity and be ready for harvesting.

▶ Radishes make a good, quick early spring crop for growing bags in the greenhouse.

Runner beans

Don't plant out runner beans until the frost is over. But you can prepare a trench for them in early spring. Add plenty of organic matter: the richer and more moisture-retentive the soil, the better the crop.

▼ **Runner beans are a high-yielding crop for the space they take up.**

Salad leaves

BABY salad leaves are really delicious, but I am not a fan of the prices supermarkets charge for them. Instead, I grow a spicy salad mix, from a packet of seeds bought for the same price but which gives me ten times the number of leaves.

By sowing a container full every three weeks you can reap handfuls of tasty leaves throughout the summer. You can sow them outdoors from early spring if you like, but they are great in 12in (30cm) pots or small patio troughs filled with peat-free seed compost.

Spinach

Sow seed of 'summer' spinach up until late spring for picking in mid-summer to mid-autumn.

▼ **Sow spinach seed 4in (10cm) apart in drills; remove alternate plants as they grow into each other.**

Winter spinach can still be picked during the spring.

Squashes

See Pumpkins

Swedes

Swedes will be ready for harvesting.

Sweetcorn

Sow sweetcorn in mid-spring in modules at 70–78°F (20–27°C) and plant out when 3in (7.5cm) tall in early summer.

Small garden tip

Spinach can be grown in any odd corner of the garden – it doesn't even mind light shade. Its large, glossy leaves can be quite attractive as a gap-filler in an ornamental border. But when you are growing the less common New Zealand spinach, the soil must be moist and rich in nutrients.

▲ **Swiss chard is very decorative and makes a fine ornamental, and productive, container plant.**

Swiss chard

SWISS chard is a meatier plant than spinach, and provides a tangier taste too. It is quite a big vegetable, but can still be easily grown in a container. The stems are very attractive, looking akin to rhubarb, but with smaller leaves; the stalks can be bright yellows, oranges, scarlet, almost purple or bright white. Every bit of the above–ground part of the plant is edible.

One way to start them off is to sow the seed in early spring in small pots or modules of well-watered peat–free seed and cuttings compost, cover it and grow it on at 10˚C (50˚F), ready to pot the seedlings up into bigger containers after about a month.

If you have a patch of ground rake yourself a level seedbed, make a drill ½in (1cm) deep and sow the seeds roughly ½in (1cm) apart. Cover them, firm them, water them and when they're about 1in (2.5cm) high thin them out so the plants are about 9in (23cm) apart.

Sprouting broccoli

Sprouting broccoli can be harvested during spring, when it will be coming to maturity and be ready for cutting.

Tomatoes

FOR me, growing tomato varieties for taste is more important than for heavy yields or resistance to certain pests or diseases. Most years I'll grow 'Alicante', with excellent sweet flavoured fruits 2in (5cm) wide, but I've also developed a liking for 'Ferline', which is quite resistant to the devastating blight disease that can affect tomatoes. 'Gardener's Delight' is a favourite cherry tomato, and also the yellow tomato 'Golden Sunrise' – it is milder on the palate, but very sweet.

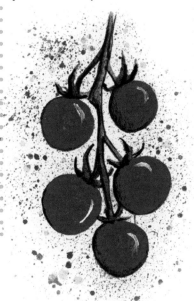

Sow the tomato seeds during early spring. Fill small pots with a peat–free compost, watering it well, and thinly sow the seeds on to the surface. Lightly cover them with more compost and cover the whole pot with a clear plastic bag or pop it into a propagator set at 68˚F (18˚C). They'll germinate in a week or so. Prick out the seedlings when they are about 2in (5cm) tall and grow them on at 60˚F (15˚C) until they are ready for planting out. This will be when the first flower trusses show.

Either plant the young tomato plants in the greenhouse or in a good sunny spot outside later in spring to early summer.

Beefsteak tomatoes can be so large you'll need to support the plants as they develop (check the individual requirements of each variety).

Turnips

Early autumn is when varieties of the winter turnip are sown. They should be left over the winter period without thinning, but from early to late spring the tops can be cut off and used to make a tasty alternative to normal spring greens. This is best done when the leaves are 4–6in (10–15cm) high. If cut frequently they re–sprout several times. And even better still, the round roots underneath will not be harmed by any of this.

Herbs

Basil

BASIL is great on the kitchen windowsill. It is a good foliage plant to look at, but this isn't the reason you should have it. The strong, clove-like flavour is one of my favourites and it's particularly suited to dishes containing tomatoes. As a plant it will be killed by even a standard autumn frost, let alone a full-blown winter chill, so basil is most certainly only for summer outdoors, or for keeping indoors throughout the year. There are some attractive purple-leaved forms and, if you grow one green and one purple next to each other, you've got the start of an indoor garden!

 Sow basil seeds on a windowsill or under cover in a greenhouse from early spring onwards.

Parsley

PARSLEY is a bright, attractive herb with green, feathery (almost moss-like) leaves; in its second year it will also produce small, greenish-white flowers. It can only be grown from seed.

 In spring, choose a sunny spot outdoors and rake the soil to a fine tilth. Sow in rows 18in (45cm) apart and cover lightly with soil. Thin the seedlings so that they are 8in (20cm) apart. Seed can also be sown in small pots and kept in a bright place.

Germination is slow, often six or seven weeks, but this can be aided by soaking the seeds for an hour or two in warm water, and also by pouring boiling water onto the soil immediately prior to sowing.

▼ **Moss-curled parsley makes an attractive container plant.**

Small garden tip

Grow combinations of herbs together in a pot. For example, chives, parsley and variegated mints look good together.

Thyme

HERBS are perfect for growing in containers, and amongst the most absorbing of herbs are the thymes. The common thyme (*Thymus vulgaris*) is ideal in stocks, marinades, stuffings, sauces and soups. The lemon–scented thymes (T. x *citriodorus*) can be added to chicken, fish, vegetables and even jam. The small but very profuse flowers, usually white, pink or lilac, make quite a spectacle.

Mid–spring is the time to plant a few in a sunny spot. Compost should be light, well drained and neutral to slightly alkaline. In summer, trim thyme with secateurs to prevent it from getting too leggy.

▲ **The common thyme (*Thymus vulgaris*) is widely used in stocks and stuffings.**

▼ **There are many golden and variegated-leaved thymes; this is the cultivar 'Archers Gold'.**

Organic tip

Keep harvesting your shrubby herbs in pots and containers: this will help to keep them in shape. Rosemary tends to get lanky, bay needs to be kept under control, and thyme can get straggly.

Herbs growing indoors should be treated in much the same way. Scented-leaf pelargoniums, for example, make vigorous annual growth and should be cut back severely in spring, just as growth is about to start.

Sum

Vegetables 80   **Herbs** 94

mer

Tips & tasks

Feeding

AFTER the dramatic growth surge that happens during the spring months, everything is still growing strongly in summer. This means that plants, especially those in containers and growing bags, should continue to be fed.

Although this applies to all vegetables, the green leafy sorts tend to survive without too much supplementary food: they get most of their nutrition from the elements already present in the soil or compost, and from the sun (through photosynthesis) – though they could still benefit from an occasional general feed with something like a general seaweed-based fertilizer.

▼ **Fruiting vegetables require feeding with high-potash fertilizer throughout summer.**

▲ **Domestic greenhouses can still have painted-on summer shading, but there are other alternatives.**

Vegetable plants that bear fruit, such as tomatoes, aubergines, capsicums and cucumbers, are prodigious feeders. They need a fertilizer that is high in potash (to promote flowering and fruiting), and the tomato foods (such as Chase Organic Tomato Feed, which has organic acceptance) will be particularly appropriate and useful throughout the summer period.

Greenhouse plants

WHEN I was a horticultural student, greenhouses had paint-on shading to keep out the glare of the bright summer sun. Today, big commercial glasshouse owners would no more consider this than fly to the moon. Computer-controlled roller blinds, or green netting on removable panels are today's offerings. But I'm a traditionalist, and as my greenhouse is of a normal size for a garden, I still use the white paint-on stuff. I like the look of the white-stained glazing panels, often smeared with white runs as they wend their way downward. Whatever your preferred shading option, early summer is the time to put it up – or on. The sun is getting much stronger now. Without shading of some form, plants will burn to a frazzle.

Soaring temperatures in the greenhouse must be avoided. Any vegetables growing under glass – predominately tomatoes, cucumbers, peppers and melons

Organic tip

If you have some unwanted gaps in your plot, you can fill them with companion plants (see pages 22–24 for details) or wildflowers that will attract benficial insects. Try nasturtiums (pictured below), which grow quickly, but beware as they self-seed very easily. Marigolds will be happy in dry spots and are long-lived throughout the summer and into autumn.

– will dry out very quickly and this can be the worst thing to happen to them when the fruits are beginning to swell.

In all cases the skins could split and, with tomatoes, there is an increased likelihood of fruits getting an unpleasant disease called blossom end rot, for which there is no cure.

Fit automatic openers to windows and louvre vents and regularly damp down the pathways, benches and gravel. Avoid getting water on plants during the heat of the day, which could cause leaf scorch damage.

Hedges

KEEP newly planted hedges weed-free, so that there is no competition for light, moisture and nutrients. Hoe smaller weeds and pull out larger weeds by hand.

Herb propagation

WOODY herbs all produce scented foliage, and can be used in the kitchen. I've also used them as edgings for my kitchen gardens over the years. They're dual-purpose – decorative and useful. None are what I'd call long-lived, and ideally they need replacing every four or five years. Mid-summer is a good time to take cuttings. Do this early in the day, when the plants are turgid. Prepare and insert the cuttings immediately, otherwise they can dry out very quickly.

How to take a herb cutting:
1 Choose non-flowering shoots that are soft at the tip, and up to 4in (10cm) long. Pull each away gently from the main stem with a strip of bark still attached.

2 Leave this strip but just trim the end so it is ¼–½in (0.5–1cm) long. Gently remove the leaves from the lower half.

3 Dip the bottom of the cutting in some hormone rooting powder, so the end is dusted. You can buy organic rooting powders but in my experience

▼ **Sprigs of woody herbs can be used in the kitchen or they can be used as cuttings material.**

their effectiveness has been patchy – so I actually prefer the cautious use of traditional powders or gels.

4 Insert several cuttings around the edge of a pot of 50:50 cuttings compost and horticultural grit, about 1in (2.5cm) deep. Firm them in and water them gently.

5 Cover the whole pot with a clear plastic bag, trying to ensure none of the cuttings are actually touching the plastic. Keep them in a warm place, but out of direct sunlight.

6 After about six weeks the cuttings should have rooted, at which point you can remove the plastic bag. Pot up the young plants a few weeks later.

Lawns

BEFORE mowing the lawn or grass strips in your kitchen garden, brush morning dew off the grass to avoid clogging up the lawnmower. Some grass weeds, such as Yorkshire fog, can be eradicated by teasing them out by hand and slashing roots with a knife.

Mulching

EVERY garden border needs to be mulched. In the case of a productive area where flowers, berries, fruits or vegetables are growing, this mulch should be made of well-rotted organic matter. It will suppress weeds,

conserve soil moisture, reduce soil compaction, improve the structure of your soil over time and feed your plants as well.

I use the shredded clippings from my twice-yearly trims of the conifer hedge more and more. Our electric shredder does an excellent job of chopping up the large branches into useful little chunks. The clippings are great for weed suppression at the back of our dry border, and they are also good for topping up a wooded pathway which currently has pulverised bark as a base. Waste not, want not! Early summer is an excellent time to apply as maintaining soil moisture will become vital.

▼ **Well-shredded conifer clippings can be used as a surface for pathways, or as a mulch.**

▲ **When vegetable plants run to seed (this is spinach), it usually renders them useless for the kitchen.**

Running to seed

YOU may see some annual and biennial vegetable crops 'bolt', or run to seed in the summer months. This renders them generally unusable. By sowing after the longest day you can reduce the risk of bolting in some crops. With some annual vegetables, including lettuce, some radishes and spinach, bolting can become a particular problem. Successional sowings can help to achieve a constant harvest before bolting occurs. Other annual crops, such as Chinese cabbage will bolt if it is sown too early, due to cold weather and the day length initiating flower production.

Biennial plants take two years to complete their life cycle and include those crops grown for their roots, such as carrots, beetroot, turnips and even onions. For these, a prolonged period of cold, usually winter, initiates flowering, but unsettled weather early in the season can trigger the same effect.

There are different ways of minimizing the risk of bolting. Spinach, rocket and cauliflower are particularly sensitive to dry soil, so make sure you keep soil moisture constant. It's a good idea to delay the sowing of cold–sensitive plants such as turnips, endive and Swiss chard until temperatures are more stable. Alternatively, sow seeds under cover in a greenhouse in modules or small pots and transplant the young plants outside later on.

Watering

WATERING should only be carried out in the evenings during summer, so that it has time to soak into the soil where it can be used by the plant roots. I've heard some people say that watering in the evening increases the chances of greymould (botrytis) fungal disease. This is almost certainly the case with lettuces, so I water these in the morning. However, it is not the case with the vast majority of other garden plants. In fact, during the summer months it is very unlikely that mould would affect outdoor plants. Fungal diseases like this usually affect plants when conditions are cold and still – and then this really only applies to plants growing under

cover (in a greenhouse, cloche, frame, or polytunnel). Outdoors overnight mould will not occur in the warmer months. As for the colder months, it is unlikely you would be watering outside anyway. Mould is more likely

▼ **Hand-held hosepipes mean you can direct the water to where it is needed most.**

to infect greenhouse plants in the colder weather. I tend to prefer watering outdoors in the evening. First, I have more time to do it properly. Second, it soaks in before the sun gets a chance to cause it to evaporate. And, if you haven't already, install a water butt (or two or three...).

▲ **Permanently laid irrigation pipes can save busy gardeners a considerable amount of time.**

Organic tip

If you are away on holiday when frequently ripening fruits and vegetables need to be harvested, then it is a good idea to let friends enjoy them rather than allowing them to go to waste. Your friends could freeze some for you!

Weeds, pests and diseases

HOE off any annual weeds when you see them. Remove perennial weeds by hand. Keep a watchful eye open for pests and diseases, so that you can take action before the problem gets out of control.

Club root is a fungal disease that affects all members of the cabbage (or brassica) family. Leaves become discoloured, the plants will wilt and, most telling of all, the roots become uncharacteristically swollen.

Once soil becomes infected, the disease can remain in it for 20 years. Keep the soil well drained; lime if necessary so that the soil is slightly alkaline. Rotate brassica crops so they are not growing on the same soil two years running. Dig up and burn infected plants, and use varieties that are sold as 'resistant'.

▼ **Club root is an unsightly – and deadly – disease affecting members of the cabbage family.**

Small garden tip

The main point to remember when growing vegetables is that they need good light, soil and water. If you can supply these things, you can grow veg anywhere – yes, even in a window-box! However, there needs to be at least 9in (23cm) soil depth – the roots have to go somewhere!

This is a perfect place for tumbling tomatoes. Or you can go for lettuces, stump or round-rooted carrots, radishes, small beetroot, spring onions, small sweet and chilli peppers and most culinary herbs. And then, of course, there are strawberries for dessert!

When plants are in window-boxes they are totally reliant on you to provide the water and nourishment. If the soil in the box is poor, then it's a good idea to add a growing compost (peat substitute or reduced-peat mix is available from the garden centre), and some blood, fish and bone to provide some nutrition. You must also ensure the plants are regularly watered as they cannot throw out deeper roots to find moisture on hot days.

▼ **Parsley, basil, coriander, mint and thyme. Herbs can make a very decorative window-box and are always handy for harvesting.**

Fruit

Apples

 By early and mid–summer, the fruits of the Bramley apple are swelling nicely. but they need thinning. 'June drop' is the name given to the time in early summer when apple trees naturally shed some of their fruitlets. This prevents any overcrowding of the trusses, and also avoids a large number of malformed apples developing, or even rotting on the tree. If, after the 'June drop', the trusses are still crowded, then assist them by thinning them out manually. With your fingers (or you can use scissors) remove the 'king' apple – the largest, central fruit – if it is misshapen. Then remove the smallest fruits and any that are damaged. The aim is to leave two apples per truss (or branch). This applies to any freestanding apple tree.

 Late summer is the season for harvesting early apples; these are the first to ripen and they should be eaten fresh, straight off the tree or kept in a bowl for a few days only. Excellent varieties include 'Beauty of Bath', 'George Cave', 'Discovery', 'Early Victoria' and 'Gladstone'.

▼ **Thin young apple fruitlets so that there are just two apples per truss.**

▲ **Blackberries are ready for picking in late sumer – but don't delay as they go over very quickly.**

Blackberries

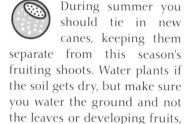

During summer you should tie in new canes, keeping them separate from this season's fruiting shoots. Water plants if the soil gets dry, but make sure you water the ground and not the leaves or developing fruits, as this is likely to increase the incidence of disease.

Pick blackberries in late summer; they will go over very quickly if not harvested promptly. Pick when the fruits are full-coloured and soft. Pull each blackberry gently away from the stem – the plug generally comes away with the fruit. Make sure you pick when the fruit is dry – if it is wet, then the fruit can soon start to go mouldy. Eat or freeze the berries as soon as possible after they are picked.

Blackcurrants

Blackcurrants are full of healthy vitamin C. The currants are ripe and will be ready for picking about seven days after they have turned blue–black in colour. For immediate use you can pick individual currants – the fruits at the top of the 'strig' are the first to ripen. If you are going to keep them in the fridge for a

Organic tip

Blackcurrant flowers are prone to weather damage, so if you live in a cold area choose late-flowering varieties, or those whose blossom can withstand some damage. Try 'Ben Sarek', a compact bush just 3ft (1m) high; or also 'Malling Jet', which is a late flowerer. This is one of the few varieties that is actually recommended for eating without cooking.

while it is probably better to cut the whole strig. The early varieties, such as 'Boskoop Giant' and 'Laxton Giant', should be picked promptly as the berries soon 'go over' if left on the plant for too long. The picked currants can usually be kept in the fridge for around a week or so, if you are not able to use them up in time it is best to freeze, bottle or dry them.

Cherries

 From early summer onwards, cherry trees are laden with fruits that range in colour from bright

▼ **Pick cherries with the stalk intact – if they become separated the picked fruits do not last long.**

red to almost black. Although cherry trees deserve a place in any garden they have one main disadvantage. This is their very vigorous growing nature, despite dwarfing rootstocks. They are best grown as a fan against a wall, where they can be controlled easily. But the wall, or wire and posts if this is your option, should be fairly high.

A good average annual yield of a mature fan cherry is about 30lb (13.6kg) but you could more than triple that with a standard tree left to grow large out in the open. Leave the cherries on the tree until ripe, unless they start cracking. Pick them with the stalk on (you may find using scissors a good idea); if you leave the stalk hanging on the tree, the picked fruits don't last as

long. In any case, they should always be eaten as soon as possible after picking.

 During early to late summer, prune cherry trees, to avoid silver leaf disease. Try not to disturb any developing fruits that are on the branches.

Gooseberries

 If you have a gooseberry bush or two, the plump, ripe fruits should be picked from early summer onwards. For some large dessert berries this is the time to start thinning the clusters. Remove every other berry and use the thinnings for cooking. For smaller dessert fruits don't thin them, but leave them to ripen and develop their full flavour. Pick them when they are a good size, but still green.

Depending on the variety, harvesting could start as early as late spring. The first to be ready are usually 'Keepsake', 'May Duke' and 'Golden Drop', to be followed by 'Careless', 'Leveller' and 'Whinham's Industry'. Gooseberries usually crop well and it's not unknown for a bush to be productive for 15 years or more. They don't take up much room, so you could say they definitely earn their keep!

 Ripening fruits will be extremely attractive to birds, so net the bushes until the fruits have reached their maximum size.

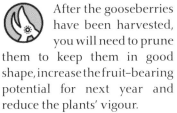

Keep your gooseberry plants well watered to achieve the plumpest fruits for harvesting during the coming weeks.

After the gooseberries have been harvested, you will need to prune them to keep them in good shape, increase the fruit–bearing potential for next year and reduce the plants' vigour.

It is essential to summer–prune trained gooseberries (fan, cordon or espalier types). Do this by cutting back all the lateral growths to five leaves. Do not prune the leaders, otherwise you'll put a halt to the normal development of the plant.

Grapes

Prune back the non–fruiting laterals on any cordon grapes down to five leaves, and fruiting laterals to two leaves beyond the fruit cluster, to help fruit ripen.

Melons

Plant your hardened off melon seedlings in early summer, in frames. Set them on mounds of soil to avoid water collecting around the necks of the fruits and rotting them. Pinch out tips when five leaves have formed.

Continue the feeding of any outdoor melons every week while the fruits are swelling. Use a high–potash tomato fertilizer. And water the plants freely, too.

Organic tip

It is sometimes said that the germination of melon seeds is stimulated by the nearby presence of morning glory (Ipomoea) plants. Melon leaves are extremely rich in calcium and make very good compost. If the only area you can grow melons in is slightly shady, this won't be a problem for the plant.

◀ **Small oranges on container-grown plants are grown more for their decorative quality.**

Oranges

I'M really fond of my orange tree. The aroma of the flowers from spring to early autumn every year is mind–blowing. Keeping a citrus in a pot on a sunny balcony or patio is quite feasible, but it will need to be brought indoors and kept in a sunny window for the winter. There are, however, quite a few things that can go wrong. Sometimes leaves and flowers can fail to develop properly, foliage can droop and leaves can turn yellow. Poor sunlight is often the culprit. New growth produced in the early spring needs sufficient time for the wood to ripen and spur the production of young flower buds along the stems. Adequate sunlight is the key to getting it all right. Make sure your plants have maximum light by moving

▶ **Properly thinned branches on plum trees are less likely to snap under the weight of heavy fruits.**

them out of the shade, but don't let them overheat – citrus plants really hate this.

Improve any yellow foliage and encourage new growth by using a summer citrus fertilizer – a winter version is also available.

Citrus plants are particularly prone to attack by scale insects which, over a period of time, can debilitate the plants. There are chemical sprays to kill the insects, but we don't want those. In fact, the brown, dome–shaped scales can be rubbed off with your fingers – provided there are not too many of them. Remove affected leaves and

then, if considered necessary, give your plant an extra boost of protection by spraying it with a Soil Association–approved pesticide, but as a last resort.

Pears

Pick early pears like 'Doyenné du Comice' in mid–summer. But use them as quickly as you can; these early fruits often don't keep well.

Plums

Do a bit of thinning of fruits in early summer, reducing the number so that those left have room to develop and receive a more useful amount of nutrition.

Properly thinned branches are less likely to need propping later, unless the tree is very old and there are obvious cracks or lesions on the branches. The wood of plum trees can break under the strain, so it is quite common to see such branches propped up. The props can be made from thick bamboo canes (the inch–plus diameter kind), or chestnut stakes and so on. With fan–trained trees, firmly tie in any developing shoots to extend the branch framework.

 During early to late summer, prune plum trees, to avoid silver leaf disease. Try not to disturb any of the developing fruits on the branches as you go.

Silver leaf is one disease for which there is a good organic remedy – the beneficial fungus *Trichoderma viride* is used as a biological control. It is also used by non–organic, commercial growers to control silver leaf.

 A plum is considered to be ripe when it parts easily from the tree. In the case of plums, the stalk usually remains on the branch, whereas with damsons and gages (as with cherries) the stalk comes away with the fruit.

Dessert plums should be harvested when they are thoroughly ripe, and will only keep for a few days. Culinary varieties should be picked while still slightly unripe, and they should be used within one to two weeks.

Raspberries

IN late summer, we have come to the end of the main raspberry fruiting season (for the summer–fruiting types). However, we can now look forward to the delicious autumn varieties.

 As soon as the summer raspberries have been cropped, prune back the old canes to ground level. Tie in young growths to take their place, and these should ideally be spaced about 4in (10cm) apart. If growth is vigorous, loop the new canes over at the tops of the wires to form a series of

▲ **Summer-fruiting raspberries are one of life's necessities; this is the variety 'Polka'.**

arches. Finally, if there are too many new growths, simply discard the weakest ones.

I train my summer–fruiting raspberry canes on a line of wires stretched between 6ft (1.8m) high posts. Three wires are set at heights of 2, 3 and 5ft (60, 90 and 150cm). The canes are spaced 3–4in (7.5–10cm) apart, tied individually to the wires with a continuous piece of twine. The canes are cut to a bud just above the top wire.

Red & White currants

 RED and white currants are essentially different strains of the same plant, *Ribes rubrum*.

Prune any bush and cordon red and white currants during mid–summer, by shortening the side shoots to five leaves.

 In most years these fruits are harvested throughout mid– to late summer. In the case of the red varieties, pick when the berries are richly coloured and have turned slightly soft. White currants should have turned a translucent cream colour and again should be slightly soft. Pick whole clusters to avoid injury to the fruit. Use the fruit as soon as possible, as they will be at their best but they can keep in the fridge for about a week.

 If your plants are just coming into fruit, it may be necessary to net them, otherwise your local birds could have a real feast.

 Red currant 'Red Lake' is an excellent, mid-season variety of moderate vigour.

Rhubarb

Rhubarb that was split in spring should be checked for water throughout summer, to make sure that they don't dry out. This is particularly important in the first year after splitting, especially if the summer is hot. Although it is possible to pick a few stalks from the divided plants in the first year, we should let the plants build up their strength. So I recommend not picking any stems until the second year.

Stone fruits

 Stone fruits such as apricots, peaches and nectarines will be ready for picking from mid–summer to early autumn. Pick as they ripen, when the flesh around the stalk is soft. Harvest them when they come away easily from the tree, but handle them gently as the fruit can bruise easily.

To enjoy them at their best, eat them within a day or two of picking. However, if you wish, they can be stored for several weeks – choose a cool, dry place and lay them unwrapped in a box lined with tissue.

Strawberries

 Early summer is the most traditional time for the harvesting of strawberries. If you already have established strawberries, make sure they don't dry out – this is particularly important when the fruits are swelling.

 Spread straw among and under the foliage of the plants now, or encircle them with strawberry mats, to keep fruits free from soil and to prevent rotting. Keep birds away by netting fruit as it starts to ripen.

 Control any mildew – greyish, powdery spots appearing underneath the curled leaves – by removing the affected foliage and spraying it with an organic fungicide.

 Strawberries fruiting in summer will stop towards mid–summer. 'Perpetual' strawberries may fruit again in the autumn. As soon as the summer types have finished fruiting, cut off the leaves to 2–3in (5–7.5cm) above the crown, and put them on the compost heap. Do this as soon as possible so fresh leaves will grow and have time to establish before winter.

If you have plants in the ground, and used straw or mats for protecting the fruits, take them up now. Weed and water the soil around the strawberries, to help encourage leaf growth. If the runners are healthy, free of aphids and viruses, leave them attached to the parent plant and peg them down, to produce new plants by layering.

It is a good idea to sprinkle a general–purpose fertilizer over the growing area. Plants will benefit from the phosphate and potash, to promote the healthy development of root growth and robust health.

White currants

See Red currants

Early summer is the traditional time for harvesting strawberries – although new varieties with later and longer ripening periods are starting to become available.

Vegetables

Asparagus

Feed asparagus with a dressing of fish, blood and bone immediately after you've cut the last spear of the season – which is usually in early summer.

Aubergines

Aubergines should be fed twice weekly with a potash fertilizer – such as tomato food – when fruits start to swell.

Beetroot

You can keep sowing beetroot until mid–summer. By successive sowing, you could be lifting beetroot from spring through to late autumn.

Pull out roots of the 'globe' varieties as you need to eat them. They should not be left in the ground to grow larger than cricket ball–size, and there should be no white rings when a root is cut in half. After pulling, twist off the foliage to leave a 2in (5cm) crown of stalks. If you cut off the leaves, the plants have a tendency to 'bleed'. Incidentally, the young leaves can be cooked in the same way as spinach.

▼ **Beetroot can be left in the ground until they are required in the kitchen, at least until mid-autumn.**

▲ **Broad beans are often the first home-grown vegetables of the season to be harvested.**

Broad beans

Broad beans should be ready to harvest from early summer. Often, they are the first fresh picking of the season, and from some overwintered plants you can often start picking from late spring onwards. Plants from seed sown in early spring can be harvested up until late summer. Broad beans are at their most tender when the seeds are about as big as a fingernail.

Pick the pods before they are too large, or else the beans will become tough. The very small pods can be used whole, but if you pick too many at this stage, the total yield of the plant will be very small.

Blackfly enjoy broad beans, in particular the young, succulent tips. One way to avoid having to use a chemical to control them is to pinch out these tips before they get infested. It deters the blackfly, and also helps in the actual formation of the beans themselves.

Broccoli

Broccoli seed may be sown in early summer, but don't leave it any later than this. Sow the seed thinly in drills ½in (1cm) deep,

▼ **Broccoli justifies the space it takes up as it is picked in early spring when little else is growing.**

in rows 6in (15cm) apart. Thin the seedlings to prevent them becoming weak and spindly, and leave them so that there is about 3in (7.5cm) between each seedling. When the seedlings are about 4in (10cm) high, you can transplant them.

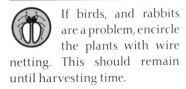 Broccoli sown in early summer should be transplanted during mid-summer. If you can, choose showery weather to do this, but don't delay too long. If the weather is persistently dry, push on with planting anyway and then water the transplants well for several days. It's a good idea to water the rows the day before transplanting the seedlings to their permanent quarters. Plant firmly, setting the young plants about 1in (2.5cm) deeper than they were growing in the seed bed. Space plants about 15in (37cm) apart, and water them in after planting.

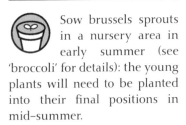 If birds, and rabbits are a problem, encircle the plants with wire netting. This should remain until harvesting time.

Brussels sprouts

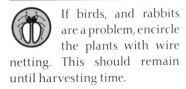 Sow brussels sprouts in a nursery area in early summer (see 'broccoli' for details): the young plants will need to be planted into their final positions in mid-summer.

▶ **Harvest cabbage when the heads are firm and have reached the desired size.**

Cabbage (Chinese)

 Late summer is a good time to sow seeds of Chinese cabbage: set the seeds ½ – 1in (1–2cm) deep in rows 12in (30cm) apart. Sow them in trays or modules, and transplant them outside after a month or so.

◀ **Chinese cabbage 'Tah Tsai' is a non-hearting variety which can be eaten raw or cooked.**

Cabbage (spring)

 Sow spring cabbage in late summer in a seedbed (for details see 'broccoli' on page 81). The seedlings will need to be transplanted later to their final growing positions. Where it's practical, cover the bed with insect netting to protect the plants from cabbage root fly, flea beetle and cabbage white butterfly. It should keep out wood pigeon too.

Cabbage (summer)

 Summer cabbage can be picked from early summer until autumn. Cabbages are cut when the heads are firm and at the desired size.

Organic tip

The tops of carrot and parsnip roots will turn green if you don't cover them with soil. These green bits will be unusable and can even be mildly poisonous.

Cauliflower

 Cut your cauliflowers while the florets are still closed and white.

▼ **If the 'florets' in a head of cauliflower start to open, you have waited too long. These are still closed.**

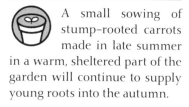

▲ **Stump-rooted carrots are fun to grow. Single roots do not make a huge meal, but mature quickly.**

Carrots

Harvest carrots from early summer, taking only what you need, as the crop will last in the ground until the autumn.

A small sowing of stump-rooted carrots made in late summer in a warm, sheltered part of the garden will continue to supply young roots into the autumn.

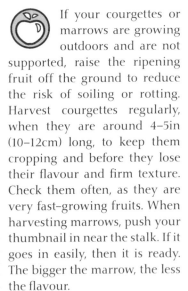

▲ **Harvest courgettes regularly, when they are about 4–5in (10–12cm) long.**

Celeriac

Transplant any young plants outside to their final growing position. Set them 12in (30cm) apart in rows 18in (45cm) apart.

Celery

Plant out hardened-off seedlings during early summer.

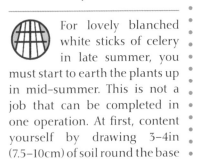

For lovely blanched white sticks of celery in late summer, you must start to earth the plants up in mid–summer. This is not a job that can be completed in one operation. At first, content yourself by drawing 3–4in (7.5–10cm) of soil round the base of each plant. Remove basal offshoots (common with celery). Some gardeners tie the stems of the plants together with raffia so soil wouldn't find its way into the centre of the plants – some would also tie brown paper collars around the stems. These days we don't usually bother – we are happy to give the sticks an extra wash before eating them. After about two weeks, draw a further 4in (10cm) of soil up, and keep on doing this at short intervals until only the blades of leaves can be seen.

Celery is a hungry and thirsty crop, so water copiously when the weather is dry, and feed with a seaweed–based fertilizer during the summer months. Any check to growth can lead to bolting.

Courgettes & Marrows

If your courgettes or marrows are growing outdoors and are not supported, raise the ripening fruit off the ground to reduce the risk of soiling or rotting. Harvest courgettes regularly, when they are around 4–5in (10–12cm) long, to keep them cropping and before they lose their flavour and firm texture. Check them often, as they are very fast–growing fruits. When harvesting marrows, push your thumbnail in near the stalk. If it goes in easily, then it is ready. The bigger the marrow, the less the flavour.

Cucumbers

 Train cucumbers that are growing in frames. Pinch out the growing tips after two leaves (cucumbers form in the leaf axils, aim for two per sideshoot). Spray and water these plants constantly to keep up the necessary moisture in both the air and the soil.

 Gather the fruits of greenhouse-grown cucumbers as soon as they are ready – leaving them on the plants too long will reduce the plant's cropping potential.

Endives

 If you have a bit more space you can sow endives in a sheltered border. These will provide seedlings, some of which can be moved to a frame, where they'll grow on with a bit of protection, while the others can be left to pick as and when necessary.

Florence fennel

 Mid-summer is the perfect time to be sowing 'swollen stem' vegetables such as Florence fennel. It is grown for its lovely aniseed-flavoured swollen leaf stalks, which form a bulb above soil level, but it also produces edible, decorative wispy fern-like leaves. Look for varieties 'Finale' or 'Romanesco'. Sow three or four seeds per station at 12in (30cm) intervals, in drills 1in (2.5cm) deep. If sown too shallow, the plants will be at risk of wind-rock as they grow. As the leaf bases begin to swell they should be blanched throughout the summer by drawing some soil around the bulbs.

 Harvest your Florence fennel when the bulbs appear slightly larger than a tennis ball.

French beans

 Mid-summer is the peak of the French or dwarf bean picking season. Harvest these pods carefully, snapping them cleanly away from the plant. The dwarf varieties produce pods over a short period – which is why it is recommended that several sowings are made during spring. The climbing forms can crop throughout summer.

Organic tip

In terms of 'companion planting', fennel is the exception to the rule that most herbs have a good influence on neighbouring plants. For example, it has a harmful effect on dwarf beans, tomatoes, kohlrabi and caraway.

Similarly, fennel itself performs badly if grown too near to coriander or wormwood (*Artemesia*).

▼ **When picking French beans, use both hands and snap them cleanly away from the plant.**

You can make some late sowings of French beans in mid–summer, for harvesting in early autumn. Sow the beans about 4in (10cm) apart in rows 18in (45cm) apart. Make sure they are watered in well, as the ground dries out rapidly at this time of year.

Garlic

 Lift bulbs in late summer, when the leaves are beginning to die down, allowing them to dry under cover. Then store them in a cool place – choose somewhere that is frost–free. Well-grown, dried bulbs can last for up to nine months.

▼ **This globe artichoke head is starting to open out, meaning it is almost too late to cut.**

Globe artichoke

THE globe artichoke is a handsome thistle–like plant, and is frequently grown more in a flower border than a kitchen garden. It grows to about 4ft (1.2m) in height, with attractive, arching silvery leaves. It's simple to grow, but the yield is small for the space required. They can be grown in a decorative border setting in a medium garden, or grown in quantity in a larger veg plot or allotment. It's a three–year crop, and plants should be discarded after the third year.

From the middle of summer onwards you can cut the heads of globe artichokes as they become available. On no account leave any on the plants so long that the scales open out, revealing a purple tinge at the base; this is the plant beginning to flower, so rendering the heads inedible (although they look dramatic).

The ideal time to cut them is when they are nice and plump, but before the scales begin to open out much. Cut the main heads first, followed by smaller side–heads.

Horseradish

HORSERADISH is a naturally occurring perennial, which produces a taproot rather like dock or dandelion. The leaves are of no value (in fact they're slightly poisonous!), but the roots are a different story.

Kale

 Sow kale outdoors in nursery beds in early summer. For details, see 'broccoli' on page 81.

 Kale sown in early summer should be transplanted during mid–summer. If you can, choose showery weather to do this, but don't delay too long. If the weather is persistently dry, push on with planting anyway and then water the transplants well for several days.

 If birds – mainly wood pigeons – and rabbits are a problem, put up a barrier of wire netting around the young plants.

▼ **Plastic and wire mesh will keep larger pests out, but an insect net will stop the cabbage butterfly.**

 ▲ **The leaves of horseradish have no real use, other than to tell you where the useful roots are hiding!**

Peeled and chopped, they are the main ingredient of the accompaniment to roast beef. If you're lucky enough to have some horseradish growing in your garden or allotment, reap and enjoy. But be careful – like dandelion, horseradish will be able to regenerate readily from roots left in the soil.

Feed the plants during the summer with an organic nitrogen–rich fertilizer such as dried blood, or sulphate of ammonia (they are natural elements but made with industrial processes, so usually considered inorganic).

Kohlrabi

 Why not make a sowing of kohlrabi? These are grown for their swollen, bulbous stems and can be used in ways similar to a turnip. If sown in mid-summer, they should be ready to harvest in about eight weeks. Varieties such as 'Lanro', 'Olivia' and 'Kongo' are good, sturdy plants. Kohlrabi belong to the brassica (cabbage) family and so are ideal to grow in the part of the plot where these vegetables are grown. Sow three seeds per station, about 1in (2.5cm) deep at intervals of 9in (23cm). When the seedlings are large enough to handle, thin them to one strong plant per station.

▼ **Kohlrabi are grown for their swollen stems, and used in ways similar to turnips.**

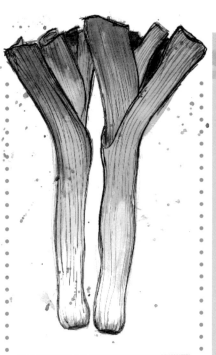

Leeks

 Leeks sown in early to mid-spring will be ready to transplant in mid-summer, when they are about pencil thickness. Use a large dibber to make holes 6–9in (15–23cm) deep and 6in (15cm) apart, dropping the leeks right down into these – but don't fill the holes with soil. Simply water the leeks in. This deep planting will blanch the stems without need for earthing up.

Lettuce

 It is not generally advised to sow lettuce in late summer, but it is possible. If it is a long warm summer, then the plants come to maturity during mid–autumn. Choose a partly shaded place as heat, drought and summer sun can cause lettuce to run to seed.

Organic tip

Leeks grow very well with celery and celeriac, and can be grown very effectively in alternate rows with one or the other. Growing leeks next to carrots seems to aid the leeks, and at the same time will help to repel carrot fly, so benefiting the carrot crop.

 When harvesting, you can test lettuce for firmness by pressing the tip of the head; but do not squeeze the sides.

▼ **Lettuce should not normally be sown in late summer, unless it has been a long, warm season.**

Marrow

See Courgettes

Onions

 Late summer is the time to lift onions that were planted or sown last autumn. They are mature when the tops flop over and the outer scales turn brown. They should be dried thoroughly in the sun, and then they can be stored in a light, airy, frost-free place. They should ideally be used before the turn of the year, as they tend not to store as long as those that were planted out in the spring.

Organic tip

Don't forget about your onions when they are drying out in the sun – if they get caught in the rain, the wetness, as it gets under the leafy scales, causes mould and reduces the storing qualities. If the season is continually wet, then dry the bulbs indoors.

▼ **Onions should be dried thoroughly before they are put away into storage.**

Peas

 Throughout summer is picking time for peas. A round-seeded variety such as 'Feltham First' or 'Meteor' is the first to be picked, in early summer. By mid-summer the wrinkled-seeded varieties such as 'Kelvedon Wonder' or 'Early Onward' are coming in. And then by mid-summer we are picking the 'maincrop' peas such as 'Senator' or 'Alderman'.

A pod is ready for picking when it is well filled, but while there is still some air spaces between the peas. Start picking from the bottom of the stems, working upwards. You will need to use both your hands for this – one to hold the stem and the other to pick off the pod.

The aim with peas is to pick them regularly, for if left to mature on the plants this seriously impacts on the yield. They store reasonably well off the plant (and can be frozen), so if you need to pick too many to cook immediately it should not be a problem – unless you're growing acres of them!

Peppers & Chillis

 During mid-summer, peppers will flower and the early fruits will develop. Spray the plants with water early in the morning to both keep the plants cool and to help pollinate and 'set' the flowers. This will also help to prevent the red spider mite pest, which likes hot, dry conditions.

▲ **Chilli peppers (these are from the 'Hungarian Hot Wax' strain) are ready for picking from late summer.**

Stake plants that are getting tall, especially if the plants are on a balcony, where they are likely to be more exposed. Most of the chilli peppers grown from seed these days are dwarf and bushy, and don't need extra support.

Apply a weak solution of tomato fertilizer (high in potash to promote flowering and hence fruiting) once a week. The results will be worth your while.

Peppers growing in the garden or on the allotment should be ready for picking from late summer onwards. But you can get early crops if you enclose the plants in cloches. Dwarf varieties should sit comfortably under the cloche, and taller varieties can be given an extra bit of heat and protection from cooler breezes by standing cloches on end to act as a wind barrier. Cut the fruits as you need them, like tomatoes. Green fruits turn red if left on the plant for a further three weeks.

Potatoes

The 'early' potatoes should be ready about three months after they were planted, which means early to mid–summer. But how do you know when they are ready for lifting? It's simple: they're ready when the flowers are fully open. Dig up individual plants as needed.

Second early and maincrop potatoes should be lifted from late summer (if you are going to use them immediately. If you are growing them for storage, leave them in the ground until early to mid–autumn). Use a normal garden fork, but be careful you don't spike too many of the hiding tubers. It's best to use a flat–tined fork, or even a potato fork (though these are difficult to find nowadays!).

Leave the lifted tubers on top of the soil for two or three hours to dry. If it's a rainy day, lay them out indoors to be aired. Make sure all tubers are lifted from the soil, or you could unwittingly carry disease forward to next year's crop.

▼ **When lifting potatoes, make sure all tubers are removed or you could carry diseases forward in the soil.**

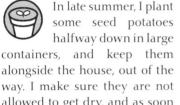 In late summer, I plant some seed potatoes halfway down in large containers, and keep them alongside the house, out of the way. I make sure they are not allowed to get dry, and as soon as the green tops appear, I put a mix of soil and well-rotted compost over the top of them to cover them. This green growth ceases around mid-autumn.

Pumpkins & Squashes

 You can still sow the seeds of pumpkins and squashes outside in early summer. Grow them under cloches to protect them from any late frosts.

Radishes

 You can still sow radish seeds during summer. They are an acquired taste, but they're certainly the quickest of vegetables to grow from seed (six or seven weeks from seed to harvest). And they're suitable for growing in a window-box or growing bag.

'French Breakfast' is absolutely my favourite variety: it's colourful, prolific and not too 'hot' to the taste. And talking of 'hot', younger radishes are always going to be milder, so don't leave them too long before harvesting – unless you like your radishes spicy!

 Cracked radishes are caused by extremes in conditions going from one to another, such as wet and dry weather. The importance of watering daily cannot be stressed too highly.

Runner beans

 Runner beans can be planted out (or sown outdoors) during early summer. Beans are usually grown in double rows, with straight upright canes and cross poles to support the twining growths. If space is short, try the wigwam approach, comprising a circle of canes tied together at the top. An alternative support is 4in (10cm) square wire or nylon netting.

You can also sow some in modules in mid-summer, and plant them out where the early potatoes were growing.

The problem of getting runner beans to set seems to be increasing, especially in dry seasons. Watering the soil at the base of the plant has a beneficial effect on flowering and pod-setting. In dry spells water when the first green flower buds appear, and again when the first flowers are fully open. Never let them dry out.

▲ **Plant out young runner bean plants in early summer and water them in straight away.**

 Nip out your runner bean shoots when they reach the top of their supports, to encourage pod-producing side shoots.

Runner beans will benefit from a mulch of well-rotted manure

▼ **Pick runner beans regularly, perhaps even on alternate days, from mid-summer onwards.**

or compost spread on the ground for a distance of at least a couple of feet on either side of the row.

 Pick runner beans regularly from mid–summer. Pods are at the right stage when they have reached 6–8in (15–20cm) in length, and before the beans inside have become swollen. Allowing even a few beans to swell will result in a halt in production on that particular plant. Only picking the beans when they are like this means that you probably have to pick them every other day. And harvesting should last two months from first to last pick.

Salad leaves

 Successional and late sowings of your salad leaves throughout the summer will ensure plentiful supply at the end of summer and into autumn.

Spinach

 You can sow 'winter' spinach varieties in late summer to be picked between autumn and spring. Spinach is practically a year-round crop.

 Continue to harvest your summer spinach. Always take the outer leaves, which should still be at the young and tender stage. The secret is to pick continuously so fresh growth is encouraged.

Spring onions

 Overwintering salad onions, like 'Ramrod' and 'White Lisbon Winter Hardy', can be sown in late summer. Also, why not try some of the large–bulbed Japanese onions too?

Either sow directly into a seedbed outdoors or into modular trays, to be planted out around six weeks later. Both types of onion will make good growth before winter sets in and they should be ready for harvesting in spring.

 Continue to pull spring onions as required, or as they get to the right size, throughout summer.

Sprouting broccoli

 During mid–summer, continue to make some sowings of sprouting broccoli, see page 81.

Squashes

See Pumpkins

Sweetcorn

 Young seedlings will be ready for planting out in early summer. Set them out into square or rectangular blocks out in the vegetable garden or allotment, not in single rows. This will ensure that the female flowers are wind–pollinated effectively.

▲ **Set out plants of sweetcorn in square blocks rather than straight rows, as this aids wind pollination.**

Space plants in blocks 18in (45cm) apart each way. I have in the past also sown the seed directly into the soil outdoors, with just as much success. If you want to have a go, sow it in early summer, setting the seeds in a block – with the same spacings. If you live in a cold climate, use cloches until the plants are too big for them.

Swiss chard

Continue to harvest chard by removing the outer leaves. Do not wait until the leaves have reached their maximum size, as this will mean that both the leaves and the stalks will be 'stringy' and tough. When harvesting, be careful not to disturb the roots of the plant.

Tomatoes

 Young tomato plants can be planted outside in early summer (if you have hardened them off). These will be either young plants that you have sown in a heated greenhouse in early spring, or they'll be young plants bought from a garden centre.

Choose a sunny, sheltered position – a south-facing border at the foot of a fence is ideal. Plant them 15in (37cm) apart. If you have more than one row, space the rows 30in (75cm) apart. The soil should not be too richly manured, and it is wise to let tomatoes set a few fruits before feeding them regularly.

Cordon tomatoes, as opposed to the trailing bush types, will need to be staked. Plant the stake at the same time as the tomato, and tie the plant to it.

If you have more advanced plants already growing in the greenhouse, they will probably be in flower by early summer. Mist them regularly with warm water, or tap the stems to help disperse pollen and set fruits.

▼ **Cordon tomatoes should be planted next to a supporting stake.**

 Feed tomato plants twice weekly with a, high–potash fertilizer once a few fruits have formed. Pinch out side shoots and take away fallen fruits.

 Spray young tomato plants with a copper–based fungicide, such as Bordeaux Mixture, as a preventative measure against blight. Although classed as a non–organic fungicide, this does have organic approval as it is a finely ground mixture of copper sulphate and slaked lime.

Turnips

 If you want to grow turnips, late summer is your last chance to make a sowing. Any sown after this will only provide green tops – which can be cooked like spinach. There are traditional varieties with cream/yellow roots, such as 'Snowball', 'Tokyo Cross' and the very hardy 'Golden Ball'. But there are some colourful red turnips, almost beetroot–like in appearance, such as 'Scarlet Queen'. They are fast–growing, being ready to eat 6–12 weeks after sowing.

Small garden tip

More and more people are growing tomatoes in unusual ways, sneaking them into every nook and cranny. They need a warm, sunny and sheltered place. During recent years tomatoes have been bred for trailing – great for growing in hanging baskets for those of us who don't have much space available. One of the best varieties for this is 'Tumbling Tom Red'. It produces prolific crops of cherry–sized fruits, with delicious flavour.

Urban gardeners with little space available have to make use of every nook and cranny.

Herbs

 Basil plants (this is the cultivar 'Marseilles') can still be bought from garden centres in summer.

Basil

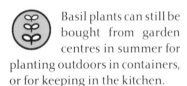 Basil plants can still be bought from garden centres in summer for planting outdoors in containers, or for keeping in the kitchen.

Chives

 You can make some late sowings of chives in late summer. The grass–like leaves can be used from early spring until late autumn. Cut the leaves to within an inch or so of the soil. Seed is found in garden centres all year round. Although you can grow chives in drills in the vegetable plot, they are useful growing in a window–box or a pot on the balcony, where you can reach them easily from the kitchen.

 Unlike any other leafy herbs, chives do not store well. The act of drying seems to make them lose their flavour. So, if you want to use chives during the winter months, keep a pot growing on your windowsill. Chives have so many uses – add to potato salad and salads, soups, sauces, cream cheese and omelettes.

Coriander

 Coriander is a quick–growing, tender herb that can be sown in containers on the windowsill and then be transplanted, or grown on and harvested from a container outdoors.

Garlic chives

G ARLIC chives can be grown blanched, or without light, to produce white blades, similar to white asparagus. This tasty Asian beauty is sometimes called Perennial Chinese Chives or Chinese Leeks (while not the true leek, this is probably a reference to their leaf blades, which look like tiny leek leaves). These finely chopped blades are great added to stir–fries and egg dishes.

 Garlic chives can be grown in pots for the windowsill, and mid–summer is a good time to sow the seed.

After a few years, when production of new leaves seems to have slowed down, you can divide them. In time they make a very small bulb that can be used like a small green onion.

 Harvest bulbs before the flower opens and it is just a bud. But be sure to leave some bulbs in the soil so they will continue to make more. Harvest blades by cutting all the way to the base. This allows new growth to develop unencumbered.

Lavender

 Harvest lavender just before the flowers are fully open, as this is when the oil content is at its highest. Do this during summer and dry some for winter use.

 Cuttings can be taken in mid-summer to replace old or leggy plants. See page 67 for details.

Mint

Y OU can still pot up mint. It is better when grown in a container, as it has a tendency to run all over the garden. Mints, of which there are many

▼ **Mints are best when grown in a container, due to their quick-spreading runners.**

forms, vary much in appearance and fragrance. Apple mint has a distinctly apple-and-mint flavour, and lasts longer into winter than most other mints. 'Bowles' mint has pink flowers, and spearmint has a sweet flavour and purple flowers.

▲ **Cuttings of lavender, this is** *Lavandula stoechas*, **can be taken in mid-summer.**

Parsley

 Parsley is best grown as a biennial – in other words, sowing in summer for using next year. Sow seed in small pots of peat-free compost for planting out into a window-box or tub for overwintering. However, their germination can be very slow and erratic, so it is worth sowing more than one pot quite thickly.

Organic tip

As well as tasting and looking good, for the organic gardener mints are perfect companion plants as they tend to deter aphids.

▲ **Parsley can be slow and erratic to germinate, so sow it thickly and in more than one pot.**

Some say that pouring boiling water over the compost just prior to sowing can be very effective in removing potential germination inhibitors but, in my experience, the success of germination is more dependent on the acidic nature of the compost. It may help to add a little lime to the mixture – but as you'll be sowing in a pot, a couple of pinches would be all that is required.

The flat-leaved French or Italian parsleys have a very fine flavour, are more upright growing and the plants are much more vigorous.

Parsley (along with chervil, rocket and salad burnet) will grow under cloches throughout mild spells in winter, providing some welcome greenery.

Rosemary

 Harvest throughout summer and dry some for winter use.

 You can take semi–ripe cuttings during mid– summer to replace old or leggy plants. See page 67 for instructions on how to do this.

Sage

 Harvest sage leaves for using during summer and also dry some for use over the winter.

 You can take semi–ripe cuttings during mid– summer to replace old or leggy plants. See page 67 for instructions on how to do this.

See page 67 for instructions on how to do this.

Small garden tip

If you missed out on sowing parsley in the spring, pots of it will be stil be on sale during summer in the herb sections of your local garden centre.

Just three small pots can be simply and easily assembled into a useful hanging basket for placing near the back door or kitchen window for easy access.

Being just green, it doesn't make the most colourful hanging basket you've ever seen, but it's not unattractive in its own way. Make sure to water it daily during the summer, particularly if you're hanging it in a place that's in the full glare of the sun for most of the day.

Sorrel

 Sorrel is a quick-growing herb that can be sown in containers on the windowsill in summer and then transplanted, or grown on and harvested directly from a container.

It is a sharp-tasting herb that is definitely best used fresh. It needs to be grown in a fairly rich, moist soil, and does not mind partial shade. Remove flower buds when they appear, to keep the plant leafy.

▲ **Harvest sorrrel leaves in summer and use them fresh; they are good in salads and omelettes.**

Thyme

 Harvest thyme for using during summer and also dry some for use over the winter.

 Cuttings can be taken in mid-summer to replace old or leggy plants. See page 67 for details. Cut out older wood by clipping – do this straight after flowering to stop it becoming straggly.

▼ **A container of mixed herbs will look good and all your ingredients are together in one place.**

Organic tip

Mid-summer is a good time to cut and dry herbs for use in the winter. The sooner the drying process begins, the better the quality and colour the dried herb will be. Hang the herbs in a warm, dry place (such as an airing cupboard), and keep them there for three or four weeks before bottling or bagging. It is a good idea to keep the different herbs quite separate when drying, to avoid any confusion or tainting.

Autu

mn

Tips & tasks

Fruit

ORDER in new fruit trees, bushes and canes for late autumn planting. Prepare sites for your new fruit plants and cover the soil with plastic to keep out the autumn rains and cold. This will enable you to plant any mail–ordered trees that arrive in frosty or wet weather. Bare–root fruit trees and bushes have an optimum period for planting, starting around late autumn, until late spring. Plant only if the soil is not too frozen or waterlogged.

Before you take delivery of your tree (or trees) make sure you have prepared the ground. Clear it of perennial weeds, and prepare the planting hole. If your soil is in good condition there should be no need to add anything to the hole, though if the bottom of the hole is compacted, loosen it a little but don't fork it over.

With poor soil, such as thin soil over chalk, or exceptionally sandy soil, dig over the whole area and improve the site with some well–rotted organic matter (manure or compost) and let it settle for a few weeks before you start any planting.

When planting up restricted forms of trees – such as cordons, espaliers or fans – install the framework and supports before undertaking the planting.

▲ **Autumn is the best time for planting fruit trees as they can get settled in the ground before winter.**

Unwrap the newly delivered plants straight away. If the weather is bad, or you haven't time to plant them immediately, heel them in (temporarily plant them in the ground) or at least cover the roots with soil, in a sheltered spot. But don't leave them there long.

When planting, spread out the roots of the tree and plant to the depth it was in the nursery (detected by the soil line on the stem); don't plant them any shallower or deeper than this. Make sure you water them in well, and then water them whenever the weather is dry – for at least the first year.

◀ **When planting restricted forms of trees, such as this fan-trained pear, install the framework beforehand.**

Greenhouse care

AUTUMN is the best time to clear out the greenhouse and give it a thorough scrubbing with warm, soapy water. If you want to avoid overwintering pests and diseases, do it now – you will remove insect nests and old bits of compost and debris where things can hide. Remove any faded leaves from greenhouse plants before they drop and attract fungal rot. Wash off the summer shading and give the glazing a clean; aim to let in as much winter light as possible. Discard spent, summer flowering plants and scrub the glass, glazing bars, benches and paths. Make sure that your greenhouse heater works, too! Greenhouses need to be warmer from now on to stop sudden cold snaps killing off overwintering crops or tender cuttings. You could invest in expensive, energy-intensive heaters, but often only a layer of old plastic bubble-wrap is needed. It is cheap and easy to fix. Even in a heated greenhouse, bubble-wrap will reduce the heating bill and energy use.

Warm days in late autumn and even winter, can still push greenhouse temperatures very high, so you must ventilate well to prevent any building up of condensation. Keep the vents free of insulation material but don't forget to shut the vents again at night.

▼ **Using bubble-wrap to insulate a greenhouse will reduce your energy use and the heating bill.**

▲ **In most gardens, hedges are used as a boundary – but they also create shelter for tender crops.**

Hedge planting

HEDGES around a garden plot or allotment are not productive in terms of food. Yes, you can have informal hedges containing elders (for elderberry wine) and hip-producing roses (for rosehip syrup). But hedges are usually functional devices for marking a boundary. They can also be used to create privacy, deter intruders and to provide a windbreak.

A good, dense hedge in the right place can reduce the amount of wind in a garden and raise overall temperatures, which means your vegetables and fruits can be harvested earlier, and for longer.

A hedge is the best option for diffusing and filtering gusts of wind. Fences or walls can create turbulent gusts a few feet into the garden, perhaps causing more damage.

A hedge also looks better and can be a haven for all manner of wildlife. And late autumn is the perfect time for planting one.

Hedging plants are typically planted as bare-root specimens, and you'll find a better selection of plants at the various nurseries found through a quick search of the internet or *Yellow Pages* rather than visiting your local garden centre.

Think carefully about the eventual height of the hedge as this can sometimes be the cause of neighbourly disputes.

Yew, privet and leylandii hedges should be given a tidy up in early autumn as growth is slowing down.

Lawns

DON'T allow fallen autumn leaves to stay on grass or pathways. Brush them off at least once a week. If you leave them they will rot down into the soil and fungal diseases will kill off the grass.

Top-dress any lawns or grass paths with a thin layer of sieved garden compost, a light sprinkling of hen manure or dried blood and bone. Brush it all in so that it is worked down to the soil level, rather than resting on top of the grass.

Don't be tempted to buy cut-price spring and summer lawn feeds and apply them now – these are high in nitrogen, which will encourage lush but disease-prone growth.

Weeds, pests and diseases

TAKE a bucket into the garden and collect any apples, pears, peaches, plums or nectarines affected with brown rot, to prevent the spread of infection. They can be easily spotted because they look so revolting! The fungal infection enters through damaged skin. Soft, brown patches appear on the fruits, and on these rotten patches raised white spots (pustules) develop. Eventually the entire fruit will become brown and putrid.

Any affected fruits may drop to the ground or become 'mummified' on the branches.

Prune out rotted fruits still attached and collect any that have fallen, burning them or disposing of them well away from the garden – not on the compost heap.

Regularly check any fruit or vegetables in store, and discard any that show signs of rotting or decay. Remove fallen leaves from around the bases of over-wintering fruits, vegetables and herbs growing in pots and containers. If the leaves remain, they will provide shelter for mice and other small animals, or if they get wet, could just turn into mush. Keep containers free from weeds. As the days get shorter, cultivated plants need as much light as possible, and overgrown weeds can soon choke smaller plants.

Fruit trees (apples, pears, plums and cherries in particular) are susceptible to damage from various species of moth that lay their eggs between late autumn and spring. The winter moth, mottled umber moth and March moth are the worst culprits.

The wingless females emerge from their pupae in the soil and physically climb the tree to mate and lay their eggs. When these hatch in spring, the green-yellow looper-style caterpillars feed on the emerging leaves and blossoms. If done before the blossoms have been pollinated this can ruin the year's crop.

To limit the effects of these insects you can apply a sticky band, or a non-drying glue to the trunk of the tree. Apply the band of grease around the

◀ **If fallen leaves are allowed to remain on lawns or grass paths, they will suffocate and kill the grass.**

▲ **This fallen apple has brown rot, with raised white spots or pustules.**

Organic tip

Although good soil cultivation is important in the organic garden, don't try to interfere with the structure of the soil and the creatures that live in it any more than is necessary.

trunk some 18in (45cm) above soil level; it halts the females in their tracks. Also, don't forget to grease a tree stake (if there is one) as the little pests will climb up these as well.

Soil preparation

CLEAR away plant debris, and compost anything that is disease-free.

Spread well-rotted manure or compost over the soil, and dig it in. With larger kitchen gardens and allotments thorough winter digging is probably called for. If clay, dig the soil roughly, to one spade's blade depth, and leave it to the frosts to break down heavy clods.

Leafmould is one of the most valuable of all garden by-products. To make your own leafmould, make a 'leaf pen' by choosing an out-of-the-way corner of the garden, knocking four posts into the ground in a square, and stretching wire netting around them. Fill the pen with fallen leaves, put an old piece of carpet over the top to stop them blowing away, and that's all there is to it. The only downside is that they take about a year to rot down sufficiently for you to use the mixture as a mulch, or to dig into the soil.

If you live on heavy, clay soil then late autumn is the best time to dig it over. Leave it in rough clods so that the winter frosts break it down further. In spring, when you want to create a seedbed for vegetables, you'll be able to tread the clods flat and then rake the surface to create a fine, level tilth. If you live on lighter, sandy soil, it is best to leave the digging until late winter.

Whilst digging, you can bury any annual weeds, but make sure you completely remove any perennial weeds. At the same time, you can add organic matter. This can be either homemade compost or animal manure. The most important piece of advice for both is that the compost should be well rotted. If fresh, it will create a noxious substance in the soil, which will kill off seeds and young seedling roots. If you are not sure where to get animal manure in your area, contact members of any local allotment group, they will know of a ready supply!

◄ **When digging in the autumn, clear away any plant debris and add organic matter to the soil.**

Fruit

Apples

The world of apples, is not straightforward. Apart from the earlies, mid-seasons and lates, they are also divided into culinary (cooking) apples and dessert (eating) apples. Add to this also the fact that in order to get optimum fruiting you need to choose varieties that flower at the same time (to aid bees in their cross-pollinating), and you can see that you need to do your research before you plant. The planting season is when the weather is cooler, from late autumn to early spring ideally, but not on a very cold day.

How do you tell when apples are ready for picking? When a few apples start to fall ('windfalls'),

then you know that the picking time is approaching. The colour of the fruit will have started to change, and inside the pips will have changed from a white to brown colour. However, the real test is to lift the fruit gently in the palm of your hand and then to give it a slight but gentle twist. If it is ripe, the apple will come away from the branch easily. If it doesn't, it's not ready yet!

Later varieties of apple that ripen in mid-autumn can be eaten straight from the tree, and are delicious. Plus they can be picked and, if stored correctly, can give pleasure well into the winter. Types that store at least until Christmas include 'Cox's Orange Pippin' and 'Bramley's Seedling'. By mid-winter, the former may go soft and the latter may go greasy. 'Crispin', 'Falstaff' and 'Royal Gala' should remain edible well into late winter.

To prevent bruising, pick the fruits from the tree carefully and place each one in a basket or box. To store for several months, keep the fruit cold but free from frost. Lay the fruit in a single layer in cardboard or slatted wood trays, or store in batches in clear plastic bags with the top loosely folded over and the corners snipped off for air circulation.

◀ **Test if an apple is ready for picking by giving it a slight twist.**

Small garden tip

You only need a balcony, patio or porch if you want to grow an apple. Okay, you can't have orchard-size trees, but a small apple tree in a large tub is a great way to grow them. They never get to more than 6ft (2m) or so in height, and remain miniature permanently. Look for varieties growing on the dwarfing M27 rootstock.

Blackberries

A few good varieties of blackberry will still be fruiting nicely in early autumn and will continue to do so for a few more weeks. Continue to tie in new canes, keeping them separate from this season's fruiting shoots. Water plants if the soil gets dry, but make sure you water the ground and not the leaves or developing fruits, as this is likely to increase the incidence of disease.

Organic tip

Blackberries make excellent edging for allotments. Not only are they productive and good to look at, but they also deter unwanted visitors by creating an impenetrable barrier, as a sort of 'living fence' or an excellent windbreak. Good varieties for growing like this are 'Bedford Giant', 'Fantasia' and 'Himalaya Giant'.

Small garden tip

If you have a smallish garden, you may have been put off growing a blackberry as they are generally considered to be quite rampant plants. However, you'll be glad to hear there are some less vigorous forms, such as 'Loch Ness', 'Merton Thornless' and 'Oregon Thornless'.

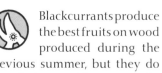

▲ **Blackberries will be producing worthwhile crops of fruit well into mid-autumn, depending on variety.**

Late autumn is the best time to plant new canes; they will have just enough time for their roots to become established before winter sets in. After planting, firm the soil and cut down each cane to a bud at about 10in (25cm) from the soil. Rake in a handful of general organic fertilizer, and water well.

Blackcurrants

 Blackcurrants produce the best fruits on wood produced during the previous summer, but they do also fruit on older wood. In early autumn, just distinguish between the lighter-coloured young wood and the older wood and then remove about a quarter of the oldest, darkest stems, cutting them right down to ground level.

You can renovate overgrown blackcurrants by sacrificing one year's crop and cutting down all stems to ground level, allowing about a dozen young shoots to develop the following year. Apply a mulch of well-rotted organic matter in spring, when the soil is damp.

Autumn is generally a good time to plant out new blackcurrants, otherwise you can wait until mid-spring. Container-grown plants from the garden centre can be planted at any time of year, but autumn and spring are the most appropriate, giving the plants the chance to settle before

▶ **Renovate any overgrown blackcurrants by cutting all the stems right down to ground level.**

the degradations of winter, or the growth spurts of late spring and summer.

Blackcurrants are useful if you have a heavy soil as they will tolerate poor drainage better than most other soft fruits. However, they do need a fertile soil – and some protection from the coldest winds. Full sun is preferred but light shade will not be a problem.

Ideally, a month or so before planting you should cultivate an area about 2 x 2ft (60 x 60cm) for each intended plant. Remove weeds and dig about 3in (7.5cm) of well-rotted garden compost into the area. Level the surface and scatter a small handful of blood, fish and bone fertilizer over each site.

On the day of planting dig a hole just larger than the size of the pot. Place the blackcurrant in the hole, making sure that the hole is not too deep – the surface of the rootball should be at the same level as the surrounding ground. Equally, there should be no air pockets underneath the rootball as this can lead to drying and the subsequent death of the roots. Firm the plant in place, and water it in.

Figs

 If you have a healthy tree, embryo fruits should be forming in late autumn. They will be in singles or in pairs. Any fruits that have been blackened by early frosts should be taken off.

Their removal will stimulate further young fig fruitlets to be produced, and it is these that will mature next year.

▼ **Fig fruits mature over winter, but being tender they need some protection from the winter cold.**

 You will have embryo fruits developing in autumn. If your tree is growing under glass it should be okay. If it's in a pot, then move it in to a garage or shed to give it some frost protection. A cover of fleece, around its base, can protect an outdoor tree.

 Potted figs will benefit from a top-dressing of fresh compost; as these plants are root-restricted, they need an additional moisture and feed reserve.

Gooseberries

If you have some gooseberries, why not take a few hardwood cuttings in mid- or late autumn? Only propagate from healthy stock, and select well-ripened shoots from this year's growths.

Using sterilized equipment, make a straight cut below a bud at the base and an angled cut above a bud at the top, removing the soft tip of the shoot.

The cuttings should be 12–14in (30–35cm) long. Leave all the buds on and dip the base into a hormone rooting powder, just so it has the merest of coverings. There is at least one organic hormone rooting powder available. I would also recommend the cautious using of traditional powders or gels.

Carefully remove the lower spines from the stem and insert the cutting vertically into the soil to half its length. It usually takes around 20 months to guarantee a good enough root system for transplanting.

▼ **Gooseberries may be propagated in autumn from hardwood cuttings.**

 Late autumn is the best time to begin pruning gooseberry bushes. Shorten all side shoots to two or three dormant growth buds. Leading shoots that are going to extend main branches,

 Prune gooseberries in autumn by shortening side shoots to two or three buds.

or are the foundation of new branches, should be shortened by about a third of their length.

Grapes

 Vines can be planted in late autumn or left until early spring.

If you have a vine or two, the bunches will probably have all been cut by late-autumn. Some late varieties may still be swelling on the vine, but there is not much point in leaving them hanging there any longer – especially if you have a cool, dark and dry room in which to store them. Cut each bunch of

▲ **The last grape bunches of the year may be cut and stored for use for up to two months.**

Small garden tip

The big issue with growing grapes is often space – a single standard vine will usually need around 10ft (3m) of growing space, whether in a greenhouse or outdoors on a sunny wall. However, there are now smaller, less vigorous varieties that can survive in a large pot for several years, with careful feeding, watering and pruning.

grapes leaving 9in (23cm) or more of the ripened lateral stem from which it is hanging. Insert the lower end of the stem into a bottle nearly filled with clean water, and containing a few pieces of charcoal. Then stand the bottle in a rack or on a shelf, tilting it slightly to prevent the grape berries from coming into contact with it or anything else, for that matter. This way your grapes should last for several weeks – perhaps even until Christmas time.

Lemons

Potted lemons (*Citrus limon*) are very popular because most varieties seem to flower and fruit continuously. To have your own supply of lemons to flavour food or drinks is just wonderful. They are thought to have originated in India, but no one really knows for sure. What we do know is that it's a plant from a hot and dry climate – not a hot and humid climate, such as that found in the Mediterranean. This means, of course, that whereas your lemon plant may

▶ **Lemons need winter protection – cover outdoor plants with fleece if frost is forecast.**

well have enjoyed being placed outdoors during the warmer months, if left outside there is every chance it will succumb in cold winter temperatures.

If you can't actually get your potted citrus under cover, then surround the pot in bubble–wrap. Hold back on the watering, and cover the plant with horticultural fleece during the night when frost is forecast.

Medlars

MEDLARS resemble small pear trees. The brown fruits are rough at the 'leafy' end and are rose–hip shaped. The fruits were widely grown hundreds of years ago, before modern fruit breeding made them unpopular.

 Medlar fruits can be harvested at anytime from about the middle of autumn onwards, but the longer you leave them on the tree, the better. Pick and store them until they soften. They are a good organic bet, as they rarely suffer from pests or diseases.

 Late autumn to early spring is the best time for planting, medlars preferably in a sunny spot.

 Prune any established medlars during late autumn. Thin out the 'canopy' to improve light and air circulation, and pull rather than cut off any suckers from around the base of the tree.

Melons

IF you're growing more than one melon plant, a medium or large kitchen garden is required. Even just one plant in a growing bag on a sunny terrace or patio can be a great deal of fun.

 Early autumn is the harvesting time, but these fruits must not be picked until they are fully ripe. There are a few indications: throughout the growing season you shouldn't be able to smell your melons, but as they become ripe many will develop a strong aroma. Also, the end furthest away from the stalk will give slightly if gently pressed, and the end towards the stalk will start to develop a circular crack. When lifted, the fruit should part readily from the stalk. Don't keep cut melons in the fridge for more than a few days, otherwise they'll be past their best.

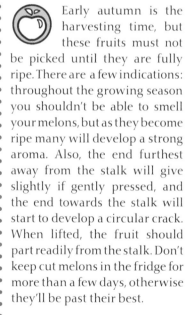

◀ **When ripe, medlar fruits are russet-brown. They are used to make an orange jelly similar to quince.**

▲ **Support melon fruits in string nets attached to wire supports.**

 In the weeks prior to cutting, the fruit will be swelling hugely. Make sure there's plenty of ventilation in the greenhouse to stop the plants overheating. And support each fruit in a string net attached to the wire supports. Ideally, this should have been done when the fruits were tennis ball–sized, but if not, do it now.

Pears

 Pears are best picked before they are fully ripe. If early or mid–season varieties are left to ripen on the tree, they have a tendency to go 'mealy' or 'sleepy' (brown in the centre) – at which point they are best left to birds and insects to enjoy. Instead, watch for a slight colour change. A green pear will go lighter green; a pear that is naturally yellow when ripe will start green and

 Pears are best picked before they are fully ripe – watch out for a change in their colouring.

get more yellow as it approaches full ripeness. Early pears such as 'Williams Bon Cretien', 'Onward' and 'Beth' should be ready in early autumn.

Pears need to be stored in a cool, ventilated, vermin-free location. The temperature can fall as low as 32°F (0°C). Fridges are suitable places to store them but only if they are very well-ventilated as otherwise the flesh of the fruit will go brown.

Pears tend to ripen all at once, so it is worth bringing a few at a time into a warmer room to ripen more quickly and make your supply last for longer.

Persimmon

THIS is an exotic fruit that is pretty much as hardy as you can get. The Japanese or Oriental persimmon (*Diospyros kaki*) is hardy to 14°F (–10°C), and actually needs a cold winter to set the fruit. Unfortunately, it also needs a long, hot summer to ripen the fruit to an edible standard. Some summers oblige, whereas others do not.

 If you fancy trying one of these fascinating plants (the dark shiny leaves also provide decorative autumn colour), then late autumn is the time to plant one in a pot. Use John Innes No 3 compost, and water it in. Check the watering throughout winter, and then during mid–spring water regularly and feed with seaweed-based fertilizer in the water every couple of weeks.

Plums

Two very delicious late plums are 'Marjorie's Seedling' and 'Oullin's Gage', which may still be picked in mid–autumn. If your tree has a batch of small plums, of whichever variety, they won't get much bigger after mid–autumn, so you'd be better off collecting them for jams or jelly. Plums picked under-ripe for cooking will keep for days, but

◀ **Plums left to ripen on the tree taste sweet, but do not keep for as long as those that are picked when under-ripe.**

 Quince will succeed in most soils, but prefers a rich, light and moist but not waterlogged place. A sunny site next to a pond is ideal, with shelter from frosts. The most suitable varieties are usually grown as half–standards or bushes. My choice of variety would be one called 'Lusitanica'; it has plenty of flesh and a good colour, and it usually sets its fruits very well.

Prune quince varieties in late autumn. These trees, or wall–trained shrubs, naturally have an irregular growth habit, and so become dense and multi–stemmed. Thin out the top growth to improve light and air circulation within the plants.

often have a flavour that is less than adequate when compared to the sweetest plums that are picked ripe off the tree.

 After harvesting, cut back dead and broken shoots on fan–trained plums and damsons to healthy wood, and shorten the shoots to three leaves.

Quince

Quince, or *Cydonia oblonga*, makes a fine ornamental tree with distinctive flowers and fruits – and it also provides good autumn colour.

 The fruits ripen from mid– to late autumn, depending on their location. The fruit is acid and astringent, and is often used for making jellies or preserves.

▼ **Quince fruits will ripen from mid- to late autumn, depending on their location.**

In autumn, after cropping, prune out any old raspberry canes and tie in well-spaced new ones.

Raspberries

Prune back old canes of summer-fruiting raspberries at the start of the autumn once they have cropped; tie in young growths to take their place. If there are too many, discard the weakest.

The autumn-fruiting varieties are easy to care for and cultivate, and they ripen in early autumn. They're very productive as well, often with much greater yields than their summer-fruiting counterparts. Pick and eat – before the birds do.

Cover up any autumn raspberry canes with horticultural fleece, and leave it in place over winter; this protection provides the ripening fruit with a better chance of reaching maturity.

Raspberries canes are best if planted during late autumn, but if the conditions are not favourable they can be planted in early spring. Here is my selection of the varieties most suited to the organic gardener (ie the most disease resistant).

'Glen Moy' early and resistant to black/greenfly.

'Malling Jewel' early and is tolerant of virus infection.

'Glen Ample' mid-season and with good disease resistance.

'Malling Admiral' mid-season, a good and healthy grower.

'Tulameen' late, resistant to grey mould.

'Allgold' (also sold as 'Fallgold') yellow-berried autumn fruiter and good grower.

'Zeva Herbsternte' (also sold as just 'Zeva') autumn fruiter and very hardy.

A sunny position is best, but light shade is tolerated. The soil should be slightly acid, moist, but free draining. Manure the ground at planting time, and mulch around the canes annually. Space the canes 18in (45cm) apart in the rows, and cut them back to 12in (30cm) directly after planting. Allow 6ft (2m) between rows.

A sunny position is best for raspberries, but they will usually tolerate some light shade.

Red & White currants

 In late autumn, all of the leading shoots on established plants should be cut back by half, and all side shoots back to 1in (2.5cm) or so from their base. This is done to encourage the fruits, which are carried on spurs at the base of the side shoots.

Sometimes, the disease coral spot can be a problem. Cut back to healthy wood any branches that are affected by it and burn the prunings.

▼ **In autumn, tidy up rhubarb plants by removing old leaves and stalks, but only after they have died down.**

Organic tip

I've grown rhubarb for more than 20 years, and my plants have never seen sight of a pest or disease – which makes them perfect for the organic gardener. However, it is a good idea when planting rhubarb to avoid growing it on ground that has previously had rhubarb on it. This means that new plants should be healthier.

Rhubarb

 Rhubarb needs a cold environment. In mid-autumn, when leaves and stalks of the rhubarb plants are dying back, you should take out the old foliage and expose the crown of the plant to frost.

 This is the beginning of the planting season for rhubarb. Potted crowns and bagged roots are available from garden centres; the pots should be planted in the normal way. The roots, however, should be set so that the buds are sitting just below the surface of the soil.

◀ **Good crops of peaches can be grown, but watch out for the main disease – peach leaf curl.**

Or you could put a physical barrier in place (which is more appropriate to trees grown against walls). Between late winter and mid–spring, construct a polythene lean-to – this has the bonus of giving a little frost protection to the spring flowers, as well.

 Any time throughout autumn is suitable for planting stone fruits. A sheltered and sunny site is essential for these trees and good drainage is essential. Add in some well-rotted organic matter to the soil before or on the planting day, particularly if the soil is thin and chalky, or hungry and sandy.

 Stone fruit trees tend to prefer a slightly limey soil, so if you live on an acid soil it might be advisable to add in some lime. (See page 39 in 'spring tips & tasks' for more information.)

Stone fruits

 Stone fruits are prone to suffering from a fungal disease called peach leaf curl. It manifests itself in the spring and summer, when many of the leaf clusters can become curled, swollen and blistered. Severe infestations can reduce cropping potential hugely, and can even kill young or weak trees.

In late autumn, just before the leaves fall from these trees, you could spray with a natural fungicide – the least harmful on the environment would be one based on copper (a natural metal), like Bordeaux Mixture. You would need to repeat this again in late winter, if you want to finally catch any of the over-wintering fungal spores.

Organic tip

The herb tansy repels flies, ants and moths. Planted beside peach trees it will keep away harmful flying insects. Garlic and chives are also helpful – their onion-like smell disguising the scent of peaches to many insects. Stinging nettles, if allowed to grow next to a peach, are thought to give the peach resistance to spoiling. Finally, the soil from under old peach trees is toxic for young peach saplings.

Strawberries

Most of us think of strawberries ripening during early to mid–summer. While this is most certainly true, there are also some autumn–fruiting types, which are known as perpetual or 'remontant' strawberries.

Popular varieties (which you can usually only buy from specialist mail–order nurseries) include 'Aromel', 'Bolero' and 'Challenger'.

◀ **Grow bags containing strawberry plants may be planted up in autumn.**

and, as with normal protected vegetable sowings, prick out the seedlings as soon as they are large enough to be handled. Plant out the young plants in mid- to late spring.

 As the weather gets cooler, cover fruiting strawberries over with horticultural fleece. This will protect them at night and keep them fruiting by creating a warmer microclimate.

White currants

See Red currants

You may be growing some of these in pots or growing bags and, if so, you should be harvesting and finishing them off by mid-autumn. To ripen the last few fruit – and to keep off the birds wanting to build themselves up for winter – it would be wise to cover them with cloches or panes of glass.

 Alpine strawberries are much smaller than normal strawberries, but the flavour is quite intense. Sow the seed in mid-autumn, overwintering the seedlings on a warm, sunny windowsill. Keep the compost moist, but not wet

Early in autumn is a good time to plant up a grow bag with three strawberry plants for keeping over winter. You will be able to enjoy the fruits next summer.

It is not worth keeping a strawberry plant for any longer than three years as it will get progressively less productive. So, in the second or third year, root some of the runners coming from the plants. By doing this every three years or so you can grow strawberries indefinitely.

▶ **Strawberry 'Aromel' is a perpetual or autumn-fruiting variety and is usually only available from specialist nurseries.**

Vegetables

Asparagus

 As the fern–like foliage of asparagus turns yellow and starts to die, cut it down to about 1in (2.5cm) above the ground. Cut up the stems into small sections and add them to the compost heap. Most modern varieties of asparagus, such as 'Gijnlim' and 'Backlim', are all–male F1 hybrids and so do not usually set seed. Female plants, on the other hand, can self–seed profusely, which can be a real nuisance; the resultant seedlings lack vigour and do not grow true. Seedlings like this should be removed as soon as possible.

▼ **Beetroot can be left in the ground until early winter; any longer than this and they can start to go woody.**

Beetroot

 If you find that your beetroot has produced a massively successful crop, then you may find you have a glut of them. You can store beets until mid–spring. Any that you do not use immediately should be left in the ground until early winter. Leave them any longer and they start to get a bit woody. If there is an early frost cover the plants with a layer of straw or fleece to make them easier to lift.

Harvest the beets on a cool day and twist off the leaves. Do not wash them as this won't do them any good. Store them in shallow boxes with a covering of moist sand, vermiculite or coir–based compost (any peat–alternative compost, but avoid loam–based types as these hold too much moisture). Keep the boxes in a cool but frost–free place. If your beetroots sprout new leaves while they are in storage, they are too warm. The ideal temperature is 34–39°F (1–4°C).

Broad beans

 Arguably the best way to grow broad beans is to sow seeds in pots in late winter and to germinate them in a heated greenhouse.

▼ **Make an autumn sowing of broad beans, sowing the seeds about 4in (10cm) apart.**

Organic tip

One thing that many people don't realize about broad beans is that they always leave the ground in a better condition than when they were planted in it! The millions of bacteria present in the tiny white nodules on the roots of the plants use the plant's own transport system for dealing with nitrogen extracted from the air. They leave this nitrogen behind, in the soil, which benefits whatever is planted there after them.

Why not try practicing 'intercropping', where several crops are grown on the same space, but which are harvested at different times. With a crop like broad beans it can be a great help to grow an intercrop of spinach, which shades the soil and prevents a cracked and crusted soil which can be attractive to blackfly.

However, if you do not have a greenhouse, you can sow them outdoors in late autumn.

Choose a 'longpod' variety, such as 'Super Aquadulce', which will withstand severe frost. It is always best to sow a double row so that the plants can give each other a degree of protection and support. Sow the seeds about 2in (5cm) deep and 4in (10cm) apart in rows that are roughly 18in (45cm) apart.

 For the best cropping results, the soil should be well cultivated and manured or compost-treated prior to sowing seed.

It is quite a good idea to plant a few extra seeds in the space between the rows, and transplant these later to fill gaps if necessary.

 Brussels sprouts always seem to taste better after the first frosts of autumn.

Brussels sprouts

 Any yellowing leaves should be removed as this will improve air circulation around the plant.

 Harvest the sprouts in late autumn, starting at the bottom of the stem and working upwards.

Cabbage (winter)

Savoy cabbages are recognizable by their crisp and puckered dark green leaves. Depending on when they were sown, Savoys

▲ **Spring cabbage plants should be planted in early to mid-autumn.**

can be harvested from early autumn until spring. These days there are quite a few varieties of Savoy, which include 'Best of All', 'Savoy King', 'Rearguard', 'Rigoletto' and, curiously, a variety called 'Ormskirk 1 Late'.

Recently, I have tried a new variety of winter cabbage called 'Chloe'. It's actually a Savoy/white cross, with bright green heads of first-class Savoy texture and appearance. The heads can weigh as much as 2lb (900g). They have a very good density, and a short internal stalk, so little is wasted. This variety can be grown at high density, so it is ideal for smaller plots and it doesn't mind the cold weather.

Cabbage (spring)

 Spring cabbage plants that were sown in mid- to late summer will be ready for transplanting into well-prepared beds in early autumn. Rotate your crops to minimize the risk of club root disease (don't plant them in ground that previously had members of the cabbage family, including swedes and turnips, growing in it).

Cabbages should be planted in rows 12in (30cm) apart, with a similar distance between the plants. Set them just 6in (15cm) apart if you're growing them for spring greens, rather than waiting for them to heart up.

 Don't apply fertilizer when planting, as this can encourage plants to grow too big and soft before the winter. It may also make them run to seed in the spring. Instead, wait until late winter and then top-dress the plants with some organically approved sulphate of ammonia or dried blood. It is also a good idea to put grass clippings between the plants, as a mulch.

 Protect the plants from cabbage root fly (by placing collars around the stems) and birds (by netting). It seems like a lot of trouble to go to but it's worth it.

Cauliflower

 Sow seed of summer cauliflowers and allow them to germinate in a frame. These will be ready for planting out in spring, and cutting the following early to mid-summer.

Celeriac

 Harvesting time can start as early as early autumn and last right through until early spring, with the peak months being mid- to late autumn. Celeriac is the sort of crop you can leave in the ground throughout the winter, lifting as required.

 The only pest that is likely to infest either celery or celeriac is leaf miner, an insect that makes burrowing holes in the leaves. Unless you are growing it as a crop to sell commercially, where perfect plants are required, this should not cause any problems for normal use.

▲ **Celery can normally be harvested from early autumn right through to late winter.**

Celery

 You should be able to start harvesting your celery from early in autumn and continue right through until late winter.

If you don't have self-blanching celery, then earth it up whenever you have 12in (30cm) of green leaf showing. Draw soil up about 3in (7.5cm) around the plants, not more. You may also want to put a collar of paper around the base, which stops the soil from getting in among the stalks.

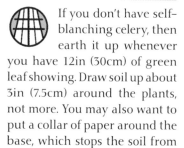

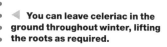
◀ **You can leave celeriac in the ground throughout winter, lifting the roots as required.**

Endives

I N late autumn, blanch endives for a useful late salad crop. Leave them in position and tie the heads of leaves firmly together with some soft string. Then cover them with a bucket, to block out the light. After a few months you'll have lovely, crisp white leaves.

French beans

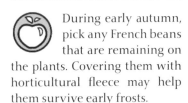

During early autumn, pick any French beans that are remaining on the plants. Covering them with horticultural fleece may help them survive early frosts.

▼ **The last few remaining French beans of the year should be picked in early autumn.**

Make a special sowing of French beans in pots in early autumn for growing on in a heated greenhouse; you'll be able to pick the beans during winter.

Garlic

You can plant garlic out in late autumn, avoiding any very wet spells. You can grow from bulbs bought from the greengrocers, but these are more likely to bolt (run to seed before the plant is ready for harvesting). They may not be as hardy either. Better, therefore, to grow from specially selected bulbs. Look out for 'Maissdrome', a French white-skinned variety with pink cloves or 'Printanor', a good variety with a mild flavour, it also has a long dormancy period, which means it can be planted as late as

early spring. A sunny position is required, the soil should be light, free draining and ideally manured for a previous crop. Split the individual cloves from a bulb and plant the largest out 6in (15cm) apart in rows. Set them about 1¾in (4cm) deep.

Organic tip

Don't use expensive garlic puree in your cooking: the environmental impact as a result of all the processing, packaging and transportation alone is enough to save a small rainforest! Garlic is among the easiest of vegetables to grow at home in the garden or in containers, yet few gardeners do. It is hardy and tough and will usually grow well in our gardens.

Horseradish

 Lift up the roots in mid–autumn but also beware that the leaves are slightly poisonous.

Jerusalem artichoke

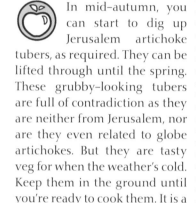 In mid-autumn, you can start to dig up Jerusalem artichoke tubers, as required. They can be lifted through until the spring. These grubby-looking tubers are full of contradiction as they are neither from Jerusalem, nor are they even related to globe artichokes. But they are tasty veg for when the weather's cold. Keep them in the ground until you're ready to cook them. It is a good idea to leave a few tubers under the ground, to produce next year's crop. And if you live in a cold climate, you could protect the crowns over winter with horticultural fleece.

Kohlrabi

 These vegetables can actually start to be harvested as early as mid–summer, but the key time for cropping is from late summer through to early winter. Pull the swollen stem bases (referred to as the 'globes') when they are midway in size between a ping–pong ball and a tennis ball.

▶ **Kohlrabi 'globes' are ready for lifting when they are between ping-pong and tennis ball size.**

You can't store kohlrabi as they start to deteriorate as soon as they are lifted from the ground. Therefore leave the plants in situ and pull them as required.

◀ **Keep Jerusalem artichoke tubers in the ground until you need them.**

Leeks

 Late autumn is prime leek–harvesting time. They are one of the hardiest of winter vegetables – no matter how severe the frosts, they will survive unharmed.

From seed sown in spring, or young plants bought and planted out in summer, leeks come to maturity throughout the autumn and can be lifted between early autumn and into spring of the following year.

Begin lifting when the plants are still quite small – in this way you will give yourself the longest harvesting period. Never try to wrench a plant out of the soil, as it will frequently snap off

▲ **To avoid snapping a leek off at soil level when lifting, loosen the soil around it with a fork.**

at ground level, particularly if your soil is heavy clay. Always use a garden fork to loosen the soil first.

One of the best things about leeks is that there is no rush to harvest them – they can be left in the ground until they are needed for the kitchen. They don't spoil either, at least not until the weather starts to get warm again.

Lettuce

In early autumn you can sow lettuce for cutting in early winter.

Choose one of the varieties resistant to milddew, such as 'Avoncrisp' or 'Avondefiance', and place a cloche over the seedlings as soon as they have germinated. Cos varieties, such as 'Cosmic', can also be sown for overwintering. The seedlings can then be grown on over

▼ **Autumn is the time to make a sowing or two of winter lettuce.**

winter under fleece (or in an unheated greenhouse). Thin the seedlings and plant them out in spring, using the tasty thinnings to liven up your salad bowl.

Sow the seed into modular trays, three or four seeds to each module, and thin to the strongest as soon as possible after germination. They should be planted out when ready, probably in early winter.

 Water cautiously to minimize the risk of grey mould fungus. To avoid this devastating disease it is usually recommended to water lettuces in the morning, so that there isn't too much water lying about within the folds of the leaves when it gets darker and cooler at night.

Mushrooms

Even if you have the tiniest growing space, why not try producing your own mushrooms? Kits are cheap, readily available and easy to use. Within just three weeks you can have your first crop of button and flat-headed mushrooms. In total you'll be able to make five or six pickings

at six-day intervals (although each harvest is a little reduced each time). You may not save a great deal of money doing this, but at least you will know that the mushrooms you get are fresh and that you have cut back on a few food miles.

There are several kinds of kit available and although they differ in small ways the principles are the same. Start by opening the pack. You'll then need to empty a bag of straw-based compost, impregnated with the mushroom spawn, into the base. On top of this you then empty another pack – a sifted growing medium (which is usually peat-based) – and water it well. Then you need to provide darkness by placing the lid of the kit in position. I check on mine every day and whenever the surface of the compost looks a bit dry, I water it. The kit should be kept in an airy place.

 For onions next year, plant sets (specially prepared for overwintering) in autumn.

Onions & Shallots

For a supply of onions next year, plant over-wintering onion sets (small bulbs) from early to late autumn. Plant them in rows 18in (45cm) apart and 4in (10cm) from each other, with each set being placed just underneath the soil and so that its neck is visible. You can use the onions in early spring in salads, or wait until they are mature from early to mid-summer next year.

Plant your shallots in early autumn. The normal period for planting shallots – in order to allow them to multiply into bulb systems – is winter. But you can plant them now for the leaves, which can be used for flavouring, as with chives.

Organic tip

You can hang up harvested onions in string bags (or old tights) and even lay them out on trays. But an attractive and more traditional method is to make onion ropes. The ripened and dried onions are cleaned up with the long, dry, yellowed leaves left intact. Each bulb is wound on to a string, its leaves twisted around and held in place by the leaves of the next bulb. Work your way up from the bottom of the string until you've covered about 3ft (1m) and then tie the top onion's leaves in place with a separate piece of string. If you make these 'ropes' longer than this, they'll get too heavy to move or hang. Hang the onion ropes in a dry, frost-free place that doesn't get too hot, and you'll be able to use the bulbs right up to mid-winter.

Parsnips

Parsnip roots are ready for lifting when you see the leaves starting to die down – which can happen at any time from mid–autumn onwards. Lift the roots as you need them, using a fork to loosen the soil. Leave the remainder in the soil for later harvesting.

It's a good idea to lift a few roots if freezing weather is forecast, and to store them in a cold shed. This means that you'll still be able to use them, even if the ground is frozen solid.

Dedicated gardeners (and chefs) know that the flavour of parsnips is improved after the roots have been subjected to frost. But why? Natural science lesson coming up: the formation of ice inside a plant cell kills the living tissue. Roots contain starch as an energy reserve, and the freezing point of starch is the same as that of water. Ice will form when the temperature reaches freezing point.

The freezing point of a sugar solution is considerably lower than that of water. The plant doesn't need high amounts of energy whilst it is 'dormant', so much of its starch can be changed into sugar, and thus provide it with 'anti–freeze'.

Hardy plants like parsnips (and Brussels sprouts) can 'squeeze' water out of their living tissues into spaces where it can freeze without doing any harm. Below freezing point they convert their starch to sugars, and then begin to taste better as a result.

▲ **Sow round-seeded peas in wide, flat-bottomed drills.**

Peas

 Late autumn is the traditional time to make a winter sowing of peas for a crop in early summer. Use the hardy seed cultivars such as 'Feltham First', 'Douce Provence' or 'Oregon Sugarpod'. The best method is to sprinkle seeds evenly through a 2in (5cm) deep, extra wide flat–bottomed drill. The peas come up more congested with a better yield for the space.

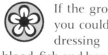 If the ground is poor you could add a light dressing of organic blood, fish and bone fertilizer.

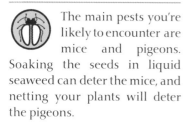 The main pests you're likely to encounter are mice and pigeons. Soaking the seeds in liquid seaweed can deter the mice, and netting your plants will deter the pigeons.

Pumpkins & Squashes

 Both pumpkins and the closely related winter squashes are best left to ripen on the plants. You can tell when the fruits are ripe: when the stalks are dry and brown and their skin is hard and bright. They should also sound hollow when tapped. If you harvest them too early they are prone to bruising. Cut the fruit from the vine with a longish stalk and leave it to 'cure' in the

▼ **Pumpkins are ripe when the stalks are dry and brown.**

sun for about ten days. If the weather is wet, protect the fruits to keep them dry. Pumpkins can be stored (as long as they are dry, clean, cool and not touching other pumpkins) for up to six months! Pumpkin flesh can be roasted or used in pies and soups, but the tastiest flesh is from the winter squashes.

Radishes

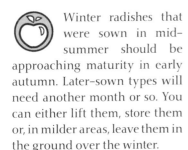

Winter radishes that were sown in mid–summer should be approaching maturity in early autumn. Later–sown types will need another month or so. You can either lift them, store them or, in milder areas, leave them in the ground over the winter.

▼ **Radishes, although not to everyone's taste, rank as one of the quickest vegetables to mature.**

Runner beans

Pick any remaining runner beans during early autumn. If you cover them with horticultural fleece it may help them survive early frosts.

▲ **Corn salad (also known as 'lambs lettuce') gives you leaves with a mild, earthy flavour.**

Salad leaves

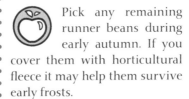

Despite the nights drawing in, you can continue to sow salad crops for use in late autumn and winter, and they are hardy enough to be grown in open ground. Better quality crops are produced if you give them cold frame or cloche protection.

Landcress: similar to water cress, this has a strong, peppery flavour and glossy leaves. It will survive being 'frosted' and you can pick it in the coldest months.

Corn salad: sometimes called 'lamb's lettuce', corn salad gives you leaves with a mild, earthy flavour. It can be grown as a cut-and-come-again crop.

Claytonia: this is a half-hardy plant with pale, succulent leaves and tender stems. It thrives on poor, dry soil, and easily self-seeds. Plants can take about three months to mature, so they will require some protection from frosts.

Spinach

 A sowing of winter spinach in autumn, such as 'Greenmarket', produces an excellent early spring crop. Spinach is full of iron and vitamins. After sowing

▼ **An autumn sowing of spinach, such as the variety 'Greenmarket', will produce an early spring crop.**

finely in shallow drills, thin the seedlings to 9in (23cm) apart from each other – 12in (30cm) is needed between the rows.

 Spinach can be picked more or less the year round, depending on when you sow it. As far as autumn is concerned you can be picking the spring-sown varieties until mid-autumn, and the summer-sown varieties from mid-autumn onwards (until mid-spring).

Spinach is ready for picking as soon as the leaves have reached a decent size. Start by taking the outer leaves, which

Organic tip

Spinach is rich in saponin (a soap-like natural substance within the plant), which is of benefit for any following crops, particularly cabbage. Spinach also grows well next to strawberries – both crops seem to benefit from the other's presence.

should ideally still be at a young and tender stage. Use your fingernails to pinch off the leaves; if you pull the leaves off you could damage the growing points or dislodge some of the roots.

Sprouting broccoli

 Mid–autumn is the traditional time for sowing crops to grow on over winter under the protection of unheated glass. This could be in the form of cold frames or cloches, or even polytunnels. Calabrese, or green sprouting broccoli, is a popular member of the cabbage family

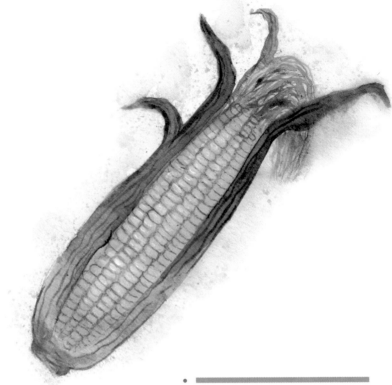

that grows up to 24in (60cm) tall and produces blue–green heads. Sown now they will be ready to harvest in early summer.

 Harvest calabrese in mid–autumn when the shoots (or 'spears') are well formed but before the small flower buds have opened. Once you let them 'flower', the spears will have become woody and relatively tasteless, and production of new spears will cease. Cut or snap off the central spear first. Side shoots will be produced and these should be cut regularly. Don't strip a plant completely, as this will also halt further production. The best spears are some 4–6in (10–15cm) long, and cropping should last for about six weeks.

Sweetcorn

 Pick sweetcorn when the silks start to turn brown. Cobs should be firm and well filled. Test for maturity by pushing a fingernail into one of the grains – a creamy liquid means it is ready. They are best eaten soon after picking for maximum sweetness.

Tomatoes

 If your tomatoes are slow to ripen in early autumn, they may need some quick help before it gets too chilly. Nip out the growing tip of each plant, and remove shoots that are trying to become replacement leaders. Remove cane or stick supports and let the stems flop over gently, supporting them with Y–shaped sticks pushed into the ground, or

Small garden tip

Sweetcorn needs space and sunshine, which a small garden often can't provide. However, a warm, sheltered spot in the sunniest possible place, with careful watering and feeding, can produce a decent crop in a small space. Choose mini-corn, such as 'Minipop F1' or 'Minisweet', both of which produce small baby corns.

▲ **Encourage late tomatoes to ripen by exposing the trusses to the sun.**

on a bed of straw to keep the fruits clear of the soil. Cover stems with cloches, so that they act like a miniature greenhouse. Continue watering and feeding throughout this ripening time because moisture and nutrients are just as vital now as when the fruit was setting. Pick the fruit as soon as it changes colour, as this helps the others to ripen off.

Cool and wet summers provide just the right conditions for the tiny fungal spores of tomato blight to spread. It is quite often passed on to tomatoes from potatoes. The disease can overwinter on your stored seed potatoes. Even tubers left in the ground can harbour the disease. Then, as soon as the potatoes produce leaves and stems, the spores spread, infecting tomatoes.

The normal control is to apply an organically approved copper–based fungicide, such as Bordeaux Mixture. Applying every two weeks from early summer will be a preventative measure to your tomatoes. Make sure you discard any diseased seed potatoes that may be lying around, and ensure that you don't leave any tubers from this year's potato crop in the ground. It'll be an effective safeguard against infections next year.

Organic tip

You can help tomatoes to ripen by placing the fruit onto some paper and then putting it into a drawer. Adding a banana will enhance ripening as the ethylene gas present in the banana is a natural ripener.

Suitable companion plants to grow alongside tomatoes include parsley, sage and basil. Flowering French marigolds and nasturtiums are also thought to be beneficial.

Herbs

Organic tip

Most herbs die back in late autumn, but you can dig up some, such as mint, parsley, French tarragon, coriander, lemon grass chives and garlic chives, and pot them. Use small pots and bring them indoors, and put them on a sunny windowsill.

They shouldn't be given too much heat; otherwise they will 'go over'. Instead, put them in an unheated spare room, but make sure you put some plastic underneath the pots. You should be able to pick fresh leaves over most of the winter.

Basil

 Basil will not survive a cold winter if left outdoors, but if it is brought indoors in pots, can have its life extended by some months. Pale, mottled or just unhappy-looking leaves may be showing the plant's displeasure at the cooler temperatures. The sunny kitchen windowsill is the ideal place to put this delicious-tasting herb.

 In autumn, you can still try sowing some basil for putting on the windowsill. Lemon basil adds a bit of zest to salads and 'Sweet Genovese' is great for using in Mediterranean-style dishes.

Sow thinly in pots of seed compost in autumn, and cover the pot with a polythene bag or propagator lid. Thin to a further pot later if required.

 If you feed your basil plants monthly, using a general fertilizer and give it a little water every other day, you'll be able to pick a few leaves each week until spring. You could try one of the new forms of basil. There are some interesting purple-leaved forms, and 'Marseilles' is a new variety with a slightly stronger taste.

Organic tip

A front door can be made more 'elegant' by having a container-grown bay tree placed next to it – one each side looks even better. And the leaves can be used in the kitchen.

One word of warning, however: bay belongs to the laurel family, much of which is poisonous. Bay itself is safe for flavouring, but make sure you identify it carefully before using it.

Bay

 In mid-autumn you can take cuttings of bay. It will take a few months to root properly (which is why it is fairly expensive to buy in the shops).

Make the cuttings around 3in (7.5cm) long and then strip off the lowest leaves. Insert them around the rim of a pot containing horticultural sand (available from garden centres; it is washed and sterilized and better than unwashed builder's or river sand). If you have a cold frame or greenhouse then the cuttings should go in here; if not, a bright but not too sunny windowsill indoors. If the latter, it's a good idea to enclose the cuttings in a clear plastic bag, to maintain levels of humidity around the leaves.

Chives

 You can continue to sow seeds of chives in early autumn. If you want to use the chives during the winter months, always keep a pot growing on a light kitchen windowsill where it is warm.

Established clumps can be divided and replanted in mid-autumn; choose a mild day, and water them in well afterwards.

Clump-dividing should take place every three years, to avoid congestion of the bulbs and reduction in plant (or rather leaf) quality. Chives are perfect for the smaller garden, and great in containers. They do best in a sunny spot, but will tolerate some shade.

▼ **Divide congested clumps of chives every three years or so.**

▷ **Cress (and mustard) must rank as the easiest of all sandwich accompaniments to grow at home.**

Cress

 Sow some cress and mustard seeds in late autumn, placing them on a sunny windowsill.

Dandelion

I'd normally be suggesting that your weed-control practices are thorough. But there is one 'weed' I have been known to make use of in the kitchen, and in France it is regularly used. *Taraxacum officinale* is the exotic-sounding botanical name – but it's plain old dandelion to you and me! Young dandelion leaves can be used in salads, and dried roots can be ground up and used to produce a substitute for coffee that is at least as good as chicory. Having a tiny area, or just a few pots and tubs, is not considered in any way restrictive by the

▽ **Dandelion leaves have a peppery taste and can be used in salads.**

dandelion as it can grow just about anywhere. If you want to cultivate it (when in flower, of course, it can be most attractive), it is best to use a large, deep, square-sided container.

 Pot it up now – pop a dozen or so pieces of dandelion root, about 2in (5cm) long, in a mixture of three parts garden soil to one part peat substitute. Water it well. In the spring and summer you'll have a fairly constant supply of leaves to add to your salads and, after a year, you can tip out the container and replant it with some more pieces of root, and a little fresh compost.

Lavender

 It is the best time to cut back your lavender plants when they have finished flowering for the year. Although books will often say to cut it back quite hard, in my experience if it is pruned back into old wood that does not show any green growth, it will not regenerate as well.

Thyme

THYME is perfect grown in a pot – unfussy and very low maintenance. Just give it a trim after flowering to remove the faded flower stems and help maintain a well-behaved, compact shape. Plant them up in pots in autumn.

Thyme can be dried for use throughout the winter. Pick a few fresh stems in autumn and hang them in a warm, dry and airy place.

Organic tip

Consider planting up a container, such as a terracotta strawberry pot, with hardy herbs. Keep it near to the back door and you won't need to traipse down the garden when it's cold, to cut a sprig or two. Evergreen types that can be harvested outside throughout winter include bay, rosemary, sage, thyme and winter savory.

Wint

er

Tips & tasks

◀ **Winter is the best time for making up new beds, or putting up structures such as fruit cages.**

a few seasons, so good old clay terracotta is a firm favourite. But beware – it's winter, it's literally freezing out there! Unless your terracotta is frost–resistant, you will end up in the spring with a pile of sharp pottery shards and a heap of soil, rather than an attractive pot bursting with luscious fruit or veg.

Check when you buy the container – many of which are imported from countries such as Spain – that it's the frost–resistant type. If you are not

▼ **There is a huge range of pot styles and shapes on the market – but choose them wisely.**

Beds and borders

MID–WINTER is usually the best time of year to prepare new beds or borders or make changes to existing ones. Do it during a mild spell, and when it isn't too wet underfoot. Add as much organic matter as you can obtain. Remove all traces of perennial weed roots.

Containers

THOSE of us who grow fruit and vegetables in containers usually like the containers to look good. We don't want to see ugly, discoloured or damaged pots. Plastic can go brittle after

▲ **Terracotta pots are susceptible to damage by winter frosts, but glazed ones may fare better.**

sure, glazed pots are usually a safer bet, although this is no guarantee they'll come through a harsh winter unscathed.

Feeding

A DRY day in late winter is a good time for applying a balanced, general fertilizer to the ground in advance of the main sowing period for vegetables. But only do this if you really want to.

The most devout organic gardeners will probably try not to use any of the fertilizers that are described below, instead relying on nutrient reserves in the ground, possibly with the addition of recycled bulky organic matter such as manure and compost.

For such gardeners, the times when fertilizers are unavoidable is when the soil is poor and it needs to be restored to health, or if the usual bulky organic materials are in short supply.

Organic fertilizers are made from animal or plant remains and include dried blood, meat and fish meal, plus bone meal and seaweed extract. These tend to release their nutrients a bit more slowly than the 'inorganic' fertilizers (such as sulphate of ammonia, superphosphate of lime and sulphate of potash), that are produced by only using industrial processes.

Always check your product labels to determine the main constituents, ie N, P and K.

Nitrogen (N) encourages leafy growth – good for crops such as lettuces, spinach and chard. But be warned: an excess of nitrogen delays flowering and fruiting,

and encourages soft, sappy growth that can be damaged by diseases and cold winds.

Phosphorus (P) is necessary for good root development, so it's good for carrots, parsnips and potatoes. Too much of it, though, will make the plants 'bolt'.

Potassium (K) promotes sturdy growth and flowering, making the plants more winter-hardy and disease-resistant. It also helps plants better withstand any drought conditions that might occur.

Greenhouses

S CRUB the greenhouse with a garden disinfectant. Light a sulphur candle to deal with pests and diseases. This is an approved organic control, involving only natural substances.

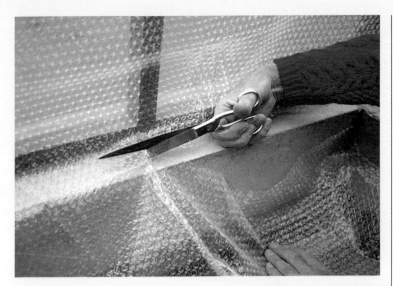

◀ **Bubble-plastic, when it is cut to shape, makes a really good greenhouse insulator.**

Lawns

ALTHOUGH the rule should always be to avoid any unnecessary traipsing over your lawns during winter, sometimes there is work to be done on them, and this is the best time to do it. If conditions are suitable (that is, no frost and no mud), it is a good time to tidy lawn edges with a half–moon tool: reshape straight sides by cutting to a taut garden line. Improve curves by using a flexible hosepipe as a guide.

Mid– to late winter is also a convenient time to level dips and bumps. Cut turf into 12in (30cm) squares, lifting them with a spade. Add or remove soil before replacing turfs and firming them gently.

Bubble-plastic is a great material insulator for the greenhouse and costs just a few pounds for several metres from a garden centre. You don't want to place heating near to it, however, as the warmth of a fan heater or oil burner could well be enough to melt the plastic!

Continue checking on both the minimum and maximum temperatures in the greenhouse during winter months; ventilate when the levels rise sharply on sunny days. The aim is to have as little fluctuation as possible.

Air circulation is needed around the foliage of your overwintering plants kept in a greenhouse. Spacing out plants on the staging or on the floor will go some way to lessen the risk of fungal infection, like greymould (botrytis).

waiting a while, you can now take hardwood (fully ripe) cuttings. Most hardy shrubs, climbers, trees, woody herbs and soft fruit bushes can be propagated this way, see page 141.

▼ **Taking hardwood cuttings is a cheap, effective – but slow – way to propagate woody plants.**

Hardwood cuttings

HAVING to buy lots of shrubs can be really expensive. However, if you have access to a 'stock' plant, and you don't mind

△ **Remove any fallen leaves from grass – but wait until any frosts have thawed.**

Continue to rake off autumn leaves, which weaken the grass and encourage worms. Lastly, help to drain boggy areas by plunging a garden fork to its full depth and wiggling it back and forth to leave good–sized holes. Work in some sharp sand with the back of a rake to prevent the holes from closing up again.

Mulching

MULCH shrubs, border plants and fruit trees and bushes with well–rotted bulky manure or garden compost, but do this when the ground is not frozen. Don't allow the mulch material, whatever it is, to actually touch

▷ **Mulching in early winter will help to protect the root areas of less hardy plants.**

the stems or bark as, over time, the acidic nature of the content can scorch the wood.

Planning

In mid–winter, compile a list of all the seeds you will require during the following two or three months, and order them without delay. Although a good many of the seeds cannot be sown before early spring, it's worth getting them early – if you leave it until later, the seed companies become inundated with orders and they will either send out late, or they'll run out of the varieties you want. Order seeds early and they will then be at hand the very second the most favourable weather conditions arise to plant them.

Organic tip

On a fine day in winter, walk around your plot with notebook in hand and look for things that should be done over the next year. Perhaps a bed needs to be made larger or smaller, or a new one created? Where to put a pond? Replace a rotting fencing panel? Which plants need grubbing out and replacing? The list of jobs could be huge.

It is surprising how heavy snow can be, so it may be worthwhile brushing it off weaker structures.

Plant protection

WINTER gusts will bring young fruit trees down, so make sure that tree ties and stakes are secure.

Wherever fruit growing is concerned, birds are definitely your worst enemy. Blackbirds are possibly the worst thieves of ripening fruit in summer, but winter damage to fruit buds, particularly on currants and gooseberries, by sparrows and finches can ruin your crops before spring weather kicks life into the bushes.

If you want to ensure good crops – of soft fruits mainly – then investment in a walk-in fruit cage is effort and money well spent. But how big a cage should you go for? This obviously depends on the size of your garden and the number of trees, bushes or canes you intend to grow. But a 15ft square (5 x 5m) is enough to grow a good combination of fruits.

Mid–winter is a good time to choose and install a fruit cage. It can be built up around existing fruit plants, or you may wish to site it over bare ground.

It needs to be tall enough to allow easy access for picking and tending your plants. It should have a hinged door that is well fitted to deny access to birds, and which should be wide enough to take out prunings. Birds can sometimes get stuck in the netting, so it's a good idea to 'double-layer' the netting with chicken wire, which birds seem to see with ease.

If you get lots of snow, it will be important for you to knock it off the smaller branches of trees, shrubs and hedges – as well as fruit cages and greenhouses. It is amazing how heavy snow can be: it can rip branches from trunks. Check that small, newly planted shrubs, such as the autumn–planted strawberries and brassicas, are stable. Heavy frost can dislodge them.

Protect any root vegetables left in the ground by covering them with a thick layer of newspaper or dry straw.

Organic tip

Various birds, but particularly blackbirds, starlings are thrushes, are a problem on apples, pears and plums, where they peck on the ripening fruits. Wasps are then attracted to the damaged fruits and will extend the problem. Smaller fruits such as currants, strawberries and cherries are eaten whole.

Small trees and bushes can be netted or grown in a fruit cage. On large trees, old nylon tights or bags made from muslin can be drawn over the better fruit trusses, and will protect them from birds.

▲ Hardwood cuttings of about 12–15in (30–37cm) long should be inserted into a slit trench.

Propagation

PROPAGATE fruiting shrubs for free by taking hardwood cuttings in the winter. This is a simple process, although it does require a degree of patience! Take the cuttings from fully ripe, vigorous growths of woody fruits (as well as ornamental trees and shrubs).

Evergreen cuttings can be taken from autumn to mid–winter, but most fruiting plants are deciduous, and cuttings from these should be taken in winter or just before the buds burst in spring. Black, red and white currants, as well as gooseberries, blueberries and grapevines are appropriate. So too are lesser known fruits such as quince, medlar, mulberry and the various hardy nut trees. Tree fruits such as apples, pears, plums and cherries can be propagated in this way, but as most eventually grow better as grafted plants, you may find the offspring from cuttings are not very vigorous or sturdy.

Start by selecting strong, healthy, ripened shoots from your established plants. Cut stems of a pencil thickness into lengths of 12–15in (30–37cm). Trim the top of the shoot with a slanting cut, and the base with a square cut just below a bud, or pair of buds. Take your cuttings to an area of prepared ground (dug, firmed and raked). With a spade, make a slit trench, no deeper than 8in (20cm), and push the cutting to the base of the trench. If you have a heavy clay soil, add a thin layer of coarse sand to the bottom of the trench to assist rooting. Leave the cuttings in place for a year, after which they can be transplanted or potted up.

▲ **Practising good crop rotation is important in organic gardening as it uses fertilizer efficiently.**

Rotation

GET the best from your allotment or garden by practising a three–year rotation of crops. Divide your plot into three strips: i) cabbages and other brassicas, ii) root crops and iii) manure–hungry kinds like peas, beans, spinach, celery, leafbeet, leeks, lettuces, marrows, onions and sweetcorn.

Over three years, the three groups are grown on different sections of the plot or garden. It is very efficient as far as the organic gardener is concerned, as pests and diseases won't build up, and manure, lime and fertilizers are fully utilized.

If you haven't practised this rotation method before, now is the time to sit down with a piece of blank paper and plan the crops, and where you'll be growing them throughout the next season.

Soil preparation

SOIL preparation in winter is important. Not only is digging great exercise, but the timing should also mean that subsequent frosty weather will help to break down the heavy clods of soil. Winter frost action is of great benefit to the gardener because the expansion of water as it freezes pushes the soil particles apart, resulting in a much more friable texture.

In the vegetable garden, single–dig established beds and, unless the bed is for root crops, incorporate well–rotted organic manure. Single–digging means simply digging to one 'spit', or spade depth (that is, of course, the depth of the spade's blade, not the handle as well!).

Work across the bed in a series of small trenches. Dig out the first trench and put the contents into a wheelbarrow.

▲ **Single digging simply means to dig to the depth of one spade's blade.**

Dig each adjacent trench, and put the soil into the preceding gap. Continue down the bed this way, and finish by emptying the contents of the wheelbarrow into the final trench.

You can dig in any annual weeds as you go, but not the perennial ones. These should be removed and left on the surface of the ground to dry out, before putting them on the compost heap. However, some perennial roots should not go on the heap as they will continue to grow and be spread around the plot (see pages 14–15).

Soil testing

CHECK the pH of your soil, especially the vegetable plot, which will be quite empty now. The pH is a measurement of the acidity or alkalinity of a soil, as described on page 39. The neutral point is pH7, and most general garden plants tend to prefer a slightly acid soil of around pH6.5.

Soil testing kits are available from garden centres cheaply. They may not be totally comprehensive on the state of your garden soil, but they can be useful in telling you what you need to do to improve

Organic tip

If you are a recent convert to organic gardening, you may well have some old poisons lurking on your shelves in the shed or garage. Check with the Pesticides Safety Directorate (PSD), which is part of Defra in the UK (www.pesticides.gov.uk), to make sure you don't still have any illegal chemicals. If you do, contact your local authority for information about how to dispose of them (usually at licensed disposal sites). Remember, it's illegal, and highly irresponsible, to pour chemicals (diluted or concentrates) into drains, sinks or down toilets.

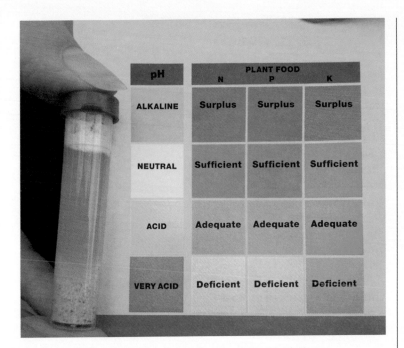

| pH | PLANT FOOD | | |
	N	P	K
ALKALINE	Surplus	Surplus	Surplus
NEUTRAL	Sufficient	Sufficient	Sufficient
ACID	Adequate	Adequate	Adequate
VERY ACID	Deficient	Deficient	Deficient

◀ **A soil-testing kit will indicate the general levels of acidity/alkalinity of your soil.**

the soil, or indicating for you which plants to grow under the existing conditions. If your soil has a very low pH (ie very acid), the use of lime is advocated to help neutralize the soil, and this is particularly important where vegetables are concerned.

Tool care

EVEN if you are fastidious in keeping your tools – spades, forks, hoes, shears, rakes and so on – clean, at the end of the year they can all do with a bit of maintenance. If you don't do this, they won't last as long and using them next season will be tougher going.

The first thing to do is to get the worst of any dirt off with warm, soapy water and then dry them. When the metal blades

▶ **Clean tools after use, but give them an extra wash, dry and oiling at the beginning of winter.**

are dry, wipe them with an oily cloth to prevent rust getting a hold. There are petroleum-based lubricant sprays, and proprietary rust inhibitors, but

in my experience the oily rag works fine. Preserve wooden handles by wiping them with a cloth soaked in linseed oil.

If you have non–painted wooden garden furniture, this too should be treated with linseed oil. But, ideally, you should then store it in a shed or garage for a few months for the oil to soak in without hindrance from the elements. Bring the furniture out again when the weather warms up.

With electric mowers and hedge trimmers, check that the cables are free from abrasions or cuts. If there are any, it is better to replace the whole cable. Alternatively, remove just the damaged part and join up the two ends with a waterproof connector.

Weeds, pests and diseases

IF your garden is subjected to invasion by rabbits – which are most active in early spring – then it would pay you to protect young fruit trees and shrubs (where possible). Guards are available from garden centres; put them in place in winter to save time in the spring.

Look for and destroy any overwintering slugs and snails. They'll be laying eggs now, so control will pay dividends later.

Several pests and diseases that affect cabbages and other brassicas can carry over from one crop to the next, so it is important always to clear dead plants straight away.

A useful way of disposal – unless your plants are suffering from club root disease – is to

▲ **Tree guards are available from garden centres: they protect the young saplings.**

Organic tip

Clearing away spent crops will not only make the area look better, but it'll reduce pest and/or disease attacks over the coming year. If you store any crops over winter, such as potatoes or carrots either in dry boxes in sheds or in outdoor 'clamps' (storage mounds), then check them over occasionally. Remove any rotting items. You can't miss potatoes infected with blight – there is a stink like no other!

bury them in a trench where runner beans will be sown next spring/summer. The remains of the brassica plants retain moisture, which is needed by the bean roots. Dig up the old brassicas and bury them about 12 in (30cm) deep. Brussels sprout stems should first be cut into short lengths and crushed with a hammer. You could even pass these stems through a powered wood shredder if you have one. When you put them in the trench, cover them immediately with soil.

◀ **Rabbits can be a pest all year round, but can be worst in winter when food is scarce.**

Fruit

Apples

A mild day in winter is the time to prune apple and pear trees. First, you need to know if your trees are spur–bearers or the less common tip–bearers.

Spur-bearers

These produce fruit on 'spurs' – short branch systems carrying clusters of flower buds. The aim here is to produce as many spurs as possible, each producing several fruits for a few years.

Cut out any of the badly placed, crossing, damaged, diseased or dead wood; and reduce by one third to half their length any over–vigorous branches or leading shoots.

To encourage more spur systems, take a healthy side shoot and cut it back to about four buds from where it joins the main stem. This will result in new, leafy shoots from the buds nearest the cut. The buds nearer the base will

▲ **Long-handled pruners are available for cutting into the high reaches of a tall fruit tree.**

▼ **When pruning apple trees cut out any old, dead, diseased or crossing branches.**

usually develop into rounder, plumper flower buds. The following winter cut back all shoots from this side shoot, to leave two or three flower buds.

Tip-bearers

These produce fruit either partially or entirely at the tips of the shoots. Varieties of apple include 'Bramley's Seedling', 'Tydeman's Early' 'Blenheim Orange', and 'Worcester Pearmain'. Some of the tip-bearing pears include 'Josephine de Malines' and 'Jargonelle'. Although some tip-bearers respond quite well to spur pruning, most

crop much more heavily if treated entirely differently. Here is how to prune a tip–bearer over the first few years after planting (if you have a more mature tree then go straight to stage 3):

1 Leave all strong laterals on the outer part of the tree unpruned until the second year, producing new extension growth. Flower buds form on the oldest wood.

2 In the second winter cut the youngest lateral wood to the top bud or junction with old wood. Fruit will be carried on these reduced laterals next summer.

3 In the third winter, and every winter thereafter, cut back all fruited laterals to leave stubs around 1in (2.5cm) long. The strong new laterals produced should be left unpruned, to start the process again.

 Late winter is a good time to check for canker on apple trees. Symptoms include an elliptical shrunken area of bark that gradually spreads outwards, and can eventually go right around the stem. Prune out the affected areas before the infection spreads, cutting back to healthy material. To preserve a branch, cut out the cankerous area with a sharp knife, ensuring all brown, diseased–looking wood is removed.

Hard frost can cause vertical splits in the bark on the trunks of apple trees. You can help them to heal by pinning the bark to the trunk with large–headed galvanized tacks. Then finish by smothering the cracked area with petroleum jelly.

Stored late–keeping apples and pears may be lightly bruised, rotting and infecting their neighbours. Check them – even if individually wrapped. Remove any which have turned soft and black and put on the compost heap.

Blackberries

 Some cane fruits, such as blackberries and other hybrid berries, root naturally when their shoot tips come into contact with the soil. Encourage them to do this by pinning them. Once rooted they can then be cut away and replanted. But only propagate from plants free of disease. Alternatively, tip–layer them into a container so you can see when the plant has rooted by looking for roots through the drainage holes. It will then be ready to be planted.

Grapes

If you have a vine and would like to increase your stock, or to grow young plants to give away to friends, early winter is your last chance for this growing year, and before winter sets in, to take some hardwood cuttings.

Take cuttings, about 8in (20cm) long, containing three or four buds. Make a cut above the top bud and another just below the lower bud. Die back is a common problem in grapevines, so check your propagating material to make sure it is green in the centre.

Choose a quiet, half–shady part of the garden, and dig over a small patch of it, incorporating a bagful or two of sandy loam. The area should be well drained. Insert the cuttings to a depth of about 6in (15cm), spaced about 12in (30cm) apart. Leave them undisturbed, to root, until next autumn, at which time they can be potted up. If you have a cold frame, then follow the same method, but the cuttings can be slightly shorter, with two or three buds. There should be a few plants ready with roots for potting up in early summer.

▲ **The flowers of the Calamondin orange can fill a conservatory with wonderful scent.**

Oranges & Lemons

I F you have a potted citrus (the commonest grown this way is either a Meyer's lemon or a Calamondin orange), make sure they are kept indoors in winter.

 Citrus plants produce their highly fragrant, white flowers on year-old wood from early winter to late spring, and they need enough warmth and humidity to flower well. Depending on the species, minimum night temperatures should range from 45–55°F (7–13°C).

The lemon, which is a little hardier, may survive outdoors in milder climates, and then if covered with fleece, otherwise a conservatory or sunny room indoors is necessary. But watch out for the sticky honeydew which drops off the leaves and onto the carpet!

 Watch out for scale insect, rubbing off any that you notice.

Passion fruit

 Late winter is a good time to plant up a new passionflower – for the fruit, of course. I'm talking about a slightly different plant to the familiar blue-flowering garden climber. Make sure you get hold of either *Passiflora edulis* (with fruits that start green and turn to purple), or *P. edulis flavicarpa* (green and then yellow fruits), both of which produce much nicer, sweeter and juicier fruits. These can be grown successfully in pots not less than 10in (25cm) in diameter, or large tubs. You should use John Innes No 3 compost, which is loam-based and has a useful amount of fertilizer added.

Support any new plants by winding the stems spirally around three or four 6–8ft (1–1.5m) bamboo canes pushed into the compost near the edge of the container. Then tie the plant stems to the canes.

Containerized passion fruit will benefit from a top-dressing of fresh potting compost. In the period between flowering and fruit ripening, apply a high potash liquid fertilizer at fortnightly intervals to assist development.

▲ **Passionflowers are highly decorative, but some forms are grown particularly for their fruit.**

 If you already own a passion fruit that is established, flowering and fruiting well each year, it will probably be needing a cut-back, and this is the perfect time to do it. Prune out the newest stems (which will have borne fruit) close to where they join another stem. The new shoots that emerge should be tied in to the canes as soon as they are large enough.

Pears

Store your pears in a frost-free, airy shed during winter months. Examine them regularly, and discard any that are showing signs of deterioration. Enjoy them the moment that they soften – at which point they have reached their peak.

Plums

ORDER plum trees in mid-winter for delivery in early spring. The self-fertile 'Victoria' plum doesn't need a pollinating partner to reward you with a weighty crop of luscious, richly

▼ **Plum trees can be too large for small gardens but smaller varieties are now more readily available.**

flavoured fruits. Some other varieties can also be planted as single trees, including:

'Czar' – weighted with dark purple plums in late summer. Fruits are delicious eaten raw, but also excellent in pies and crumbles. Its flowers are frost-resistant, which can be a real bonus if you live in a cold part of the country.

'Jubilee' – a relative newcomer, it is similar to 'Victoria' but ripening a week or so earlier (in mid-summer). Its fruits are also a little larger.

'Marjorie's Seedling' – is ready for picking in early autumn, with large, purplish and sweetly flavoured plums. Good raw or for stewing.

Raspberries

 In late winter, if you haven't already done it, shorten all canes of autumn-fruiting raspberries to within 1in (2.5cm) of the ground, to stimulate the production of new shoots which will crop from early autumn.

Plant raspberries 15in (37cm) apart in rows 5ft (1.5m) apart, in some manured soil. Shorten the canes to just above a bud about 9in (23cm) from the base.

▼ **For succulent summer raspberries you should prune – and perhaps plant – in winter.**

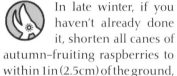

Rhubarb

Forcing your rhubarb in winter provides you with earlier crops of tender pink stalks. Harvest as early as late winter (if forced indoors), or from early spring (when forced in situ).

If you want early stalks, dig up a strong clump in winter, and place it in a box, packing the roots in closely. Cover the crown with a thin layer of soil, and water it well. Place a black bin liner over the top, to exclude all light. Keep the box in a warm greenhouse or shed, at about 50–55°F (10–13°C). You should be able to pull the sticks in four or five weeks.

Plant rhubarb crowns throughout winter, as long as the soil isn't frozen or waterlogged.

▲ **Forced rhubarb provides tender young stalks from late winter onwards.**

▼ **When harvesting rhubarb, pull it gently from the crown, don't cut it.**

Stone fruits

Peach leaf curl is a fungal disease leading to the disfigurement of peach, nectarine, apricot and almond leaves. In small gardens it can affect fan–trained trees.

The leaves become blistered, bright red or purple, before they eventually fall prematurely, reducing the vigour of the tree. As well as spraying with an organically approved fungicide containing copper (as suggested back in autumn), you can also spray in late winter as the buds swell, and do this again about a fortnight later.

You can also help prevent peach leaf curl by keeping the tree's branches dry over winter. Erect a clear polythene rainproof cover over them, putting it up now and leaving it in place until spring. Don't let the cover touch the plant, and ensure that it's in contact with the soil. Remove it, or at least ventilate it, on warm sunny days.

Strawberries

For great strawberries in summer, you may need to give the plants a little attention in late winter. If your soil is particularly hungry, it would be a good idea to feed the plants with sulphate of potash, applied to the soil or compost, at a rate of ½oz per sq yd (15g per m²). Maximum crops are had from plants where the leaves are pale green, so it's best to avoid compound fertilizers that contain lots of nitrogen (which promotes leaf growth), unless the vigour of the plants is causing concern.

During early winter, bring some potted strawberries into the greenhouse. It should be heated during the coldest parts of the winter (maintaining a minimum of 46°F or 7°C). These plants will develop flowers over late winter and start fruiting in early spring. Any of the outside varieties will do well in the greenhouse, but some varieties are particularly recommended for their early cropping. These include 'Royal Sovereign' – arguably the best-tasting strawberry of all.

Shield strawberries from icy winds by covering them with cloches in winter; seal both ends of the cloches to avoid creating a wind tunnel. When flowers appear move alternate cloches away, so that bees and pollinating insects have access.

◀ **Peach leaf curl is a fungal disease, which is thought to be spread via spores in rainwater.**

Organic tip

If you are undertaking some winter planning, and wanting to locate the ideal place for growing strawberries, arrange it so that they grow near to dwarf beans, lettuce, spinach and especially borage. They also do well near to a spruce hedge (but they should not be shaded by it). Note that they perform very badly, however, if sited next to cabbage!

Vegetables

Brussels sprouts

Early winter is the height of the Brussels sprout season, and plants need checking every few days as the sprouts quickly harden and mature. For me, the best-tasting sprouts are the ones that have had some winter frost on them. The first sprouts of the year, from mid-autumn, are usually bland when compared to winter-picked types that have been out in the cold for longer. The act of freezing the cells seems to increase the sugary content within them and it gives the button sprouts a much

Asparagus

▲ **Yellowing asparagus foliage should be cut back to about 2–3in (5–7.5cm) in autumn or winter.**

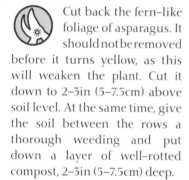
Cut back the fern-like foliage of asparagus. It should not be removed before it turns yellow, as this will weaken the plant. Cut it down to 2–3in (5–7.5cm) above soil level. At the same time, give the soil between the rows a thorough weeding and put down a layer of well-rotted compost, 2–3in (5–7.5cm) deep.

Broad beans

Sow broad beans, such as 'Express' or 'Witkiem Manita' in pots in the greenhouse in late winter.

▶ **Often the first vegetable of the year to be harvested, the broad bean, is from a late winter sowing.**

nuttier flavour. See also parsnips, page 124. Pick or cut the sprouts from the bottom upwards, and cut off the leafy plant tops for use as winter greens. Many modern hybrid sprout varieties are designed for complete harvest at a single picking. So, if the weather turns cold, you can pull up a few mature plants and take them indoors to strip the stems in comfort. Or hang up a few reserve plants in a cool shed to keep for a week or two until they're needed.

 If your Brussels sprout plants are looking a little unkempt, remove yellowing leaves from the stems, as these serve no beneficial purpose to the plant. Doing this also helps to improve the air circulation in and around the developing sprouts.

Cabbage (spring)

 Spring cabbage will be needing a feed in late winter; a gentle sprinkling of fish, blood and bone meal will boost growth and help it to 'heart up'.

 Do not forget to net young cabbage plants against pigeons. If you don't, the birds can quickly shred the plants.

Carrots

 Sow the forcing carrot 'Amsterdam' in a cold frame or growing bag in the greenhouse. This will give you the earliest crops next year. Make sowings every two weeks through winter.

Late winter is the time to order seeds so that they arrive in good time for the earliest sowings to take place in spring.

A good choice is to grow naturally resistant varieties to carrot fly, such as 'Fly Away F1' and 'Resistafly F1'. It has to be said that these are not 100% resistant, and a small attack may occur. For absolutely the best results, grow one of these two resistant varieties alongside a non-resistant variety (such as 'Chantenay'). This will allow any carrot fly in your area to attack the non-resistant row, and leave the others clean. You can also confuse the fly by sowing flowers such as the annual flax (*Linum rubrum*) next to your carrots. This seems to deflect the carrots' scent, which is what lures the fly in.

◀ **When harvesting Brussels sprouts, work from the bottom of the plant upwards.**

▶ **Plant chicory roots in a large pot and keep them in the dark; they'll produce tasty, tender 'chicons'.**

Cauliflower

 Do not let frost and bitter winds damage any cauliflower curds. Cover them loosely with fleece, or use a few of the plant's leaves, kept in place with twine.

As with cabbages, kale, broccoli, calabrese and Chinese greens, don't forget to net cauliflowers against pigeons.

Cauliflower is a crop that can often be cut practically all the year round. Varieties that can be harvested in late winter were sown outdoors during the previous early summer and transplanted a month later. Begin harvesting some of them while they are still fairly small, rather than waiting for them all to mature and produce a glut. You have waited too long if the florets have started to separate.

Cut them in the morning when the heads still have dew on them, but in frosty weather wait until midday. If you wish to keep the heads for up to three weeks before using them, lift the plants, shake the soil from the roots and hang them upside down in a cool shed. It is a good idea to mist the curds occasionally to keep them fresh.

Chicory

'Witloof" chicory is an ornamental vegetable with a rosette of leaves and a deep root. It is grown for its tight conical buds of young white leaves, called 'chicons'. Best results are obtained by forcing roots in the dark in winter (indoors or in pots), after lifting them from the open ground. Plant six roots in a 8–9in (20–23cm) diameter pot filled with a mix of moist soil and

▶ **Netting over any form of brassica to protect against pigeon damage is an important winter measure.**

sand, with ½–¾in (1–2cm) of crown above the surface. Place a similar pot over the top, and block out light from the drainage holes. Store in an airing cupboard, or other dark, warm place. Water if the soil dries out. Harvest after ten weeks.

Endives

ENDIVE is a hardy annual, closely related to chicory. It is used as a salad leaf, but it needs to be blanched for it to be palatable. It needs a light soil and an open position, although it will usefully withstand some partial shade.

 Endive seed can be sown from late winter onwards, and batches can continue to be sown every three or four weeks until late summer. Sow seed thinly in drills ½in (1cm) deep and 12in (30cm) apart, and when the seedlings are large enough to handle, thin them out to 9–12in (23–30cm) apart. When the plants are fully grown, some 12–14 weeks after sowing, you should blanch them.

With raffia or soft twine, loosely tie the fully grown leaves together and then cover the plant with a large upside-down pot. Cover the drainage holes to exclude all light.

After about three weeks, when the leaves are creamy white, cut the plants off just above soil level with a sharp knife. The resulting leaves will be tangy without being bitter.

Small garden tip

I even grow a few endives in pots for the patio – they're easier to blanch, as all you need to do is invert a pot over the top of the growing container.

▼ **Fully grown endive leaves should be blanched – by being tied together and having a pot inverted over them.**

Lettuce

 In winter you can sow some cut-and-come-again lettuce thinly in rows. With these crops, instead of harvesting the whole plant, just cut off the leaves as needed, leaving the rest of the plant to grow on. You can sow seeds straight into the ground, as long as you protect them from the weather by covering them with fleece, or sowing them into a cold frame. Gather the leaves as soon as they are usable. You can also sow some hearting lettuce, treating them the same way.

Mushrooms

 You can still continue growing mushrooms in kits, see page 123.

Okra

 Late winter is a good time to sow okra seed. You can start them off on a bright kitchen windowsill or warm conservatory. Okra is naturally a tropical plant, and in colder climates you'll be able to grow it outdoors in a sunny spot in a container – but it's only in the longer, hotter summers when you'll get the best fruits to pick. Seedlings will need to be pricked out and potted on a couple of times during the spring months until early summer, when you'll be able to plant them up into tubs or growbags. 'Burgundy Red' and 'Clemson's Spineless are excellent.

Onions & Shallots

 Shallot bulbs are available from garden centres in late winter, or from mail order seed companies. Grow them one year and you can even save some at the end of the season for planting the following year – for free! Each bulb has the potential to produce up to ten similar-sized 'offsets' by the end of the growing season – that's a 100% return on your investment. They do best in well-drained soil, or in a pot of soil-based compost; they don't like freshly manured soil. Some of the best varieties for good flavour are: 'Topper', 'Mikor' and 'Pikant'.

 For really firm bulbs, feed them with some potash. You can apply a granular fertilizer based on poultry manure at about 2–3oz (60–90g) per sq yard/metre.

Small garden tip

If you only have a small patch of garden it's unlikely you'll easily find room for a row of onions. Shallots, however, are a much better bet. Their flavour is milder than that of onions, and they're easier to grow, too. Both types of crop are, however, suitable for growing in containers.

 If parsnips are still in the ground by late winter you should lift them and store them in boxes.

 Next year's parsnips can be sown as early as late winter right through until mid–spring.

Potatoes

 Seed potatoes that were planted in late summer are ready for harvesting in early winter, and this late potato crop is all about quality, not quantity.

You can start to chit (sprout) potatoes in late winter by setting seed tubers eye–end upwards in egg cartons or shallow trays in a cool, light place – a spare room is ideal. See page 58 for details.

Parsnips

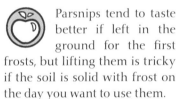 Parsnips tend to taste better if left in the ground for the first frosts, but lifting them is tricky if the soil is solid with frost on the day you want to use them.

So, a few days beforehand, when the soil is unfrozen, gently pull some parsnips and move them closer to the house. Make a shallow drill, either in the open ground or in a container, and lay the parsnips on their sides inside. Then cover them over with soil.

The top leaves of parsnips will have died back by now, so as you lay the roots in the drill, make sure the tips of the roots are protruding from the soil so that you can identify their positions. By doing this, if there is a frost, the parsnips will be easy to lift.

If you still have some remaining parsnips in their original sowing positions by late winter, then lift them and store them in boxes, for using as soon as possible. They will not improve if you leave them in the ground, and will be susceptible to pests.

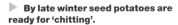 **By late winter seed potatoes are ready for 'chitting'.**

Radishes

 Radish seeds can be sown into pots and containers in a light, open compost in late winter. Sow the seed ½in (1cm) deep and place the container in a sunny spot. When the seedlings are large enough to handle, thin them to at least 1in (2.5cm) apart, with sufficient space to ensure they are not too overcrowded. Harvest them as soon as the roots are large enough – at this time of year that should be in ten weeks or so.

Runner beans

 Where you intend to grow runner beans, late winter is the time to prepare the soil. Dig a trench 12in (30cm) deep and 18in (45cm) wide. Bank up the soil on either side. Between now and sowing time in spring, three-quarters fill the trench with well-rotted organic matter. Leave it open, but put in the organic matter as and when it becomes available.

 Spinach is one of the easiest, healthiest and most versatile of vegetables any gardener could grow.

Spinach

 Continue to harvest spinach throughout winter. If you live in a particularly cold area, covering the rows with cloches can protect the plants and keep them clean.

Organic tip

Tomato growers keen on companion planting will have masses of opportunities: tomatoes and asparagus, and tomatoes and parsley are both mutually helpful. Also, growing tomatoes with any members of the cabbage family will help to ward off the white cabbage butterfly.

Many pests seem to leave gooseberries alone if tomatoes are grown close by. But don't grow tomatoes near to apricots, as neither will do well.

▲ **Although they are hot-climate plants, tomatoes can be sown in mid-winter with care and attention.**

Tomatoes

You may be thinking to yourself, 'Tomatoes are tropical plants – you can't possibly sow them in the depths of winter!' You'd be half right. They are, but you can! You'll need a greenhouse heated to a minimum night temperature of 50–56°F (10–13°C). Fill a seed tray with some peat–free sowing compost. Tomato seeds are large enough to handle individually, so gently push one into the compost, spacing them about ¾in (2cm) apart each way. Cover them by pushing the compost over the top. The seed should only be about ¼in (6mm) deep. Cover the tray with a polythene bag and place it in the heated greenhouse. Even better, pop the tray into a propagator unit if you have one.

Germination should take place in 8–11 days, depending on the heat available. When the seedlings are clearly visible, remove the cover. After three or four weeks the young plants will need potting up into 3in (7.5cm) pots. In mid–spring they can then be planted into their fruiting places: the greenhouse border or into growing bags to be kept under glass. Depending on the sunshine levels this spring, you could even get fruits to ripen by early summer, and certainly by mid–summer – much earlier than later–sown tomatoes.

Any variety of cherry tomato can be grown in this way. Try: 'Mini Charm' (very sweet, mini–plum–shaped fruits on long trusses); 'Bistro F1' (masses of cherry–sized fruits, best eaten straight from the vine); and then 'Gardeners Delight' (heavy cropping and long lasting).

Herbs

Bay

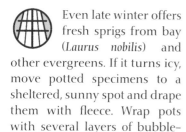

Even late winter offers fresh sprigs from bay (*Laurus nobilis*) and other evergreens. If it turns icy, move potted specimens to a sheltered, sunny spot and drape them with fleece. Wrap pots with several layers of bubble-plastic to insulate roots from biting frosts.

Bay trees will need trimming to help keep them in shape. There is no right or wrong time to do this, so I aim to get it done in late winter, to avoid having to do it when it's busier in the garden!

Chives

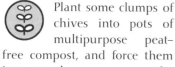

Plant some clumps of chives into pots of multipurpose peat-free compost, and force them into growth on a warm, south-facing windowsill.

Cress

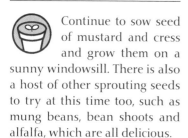

Continue to sow seed of mustard and cress and grow them on a sunny windowsill. There is also a host of other sprouting seeds to try at this time too, such as mung beans, bean shoots and alfalfa, which are all delicious.

▲ **Plant individual garlic cloves with the basal plate at the bottom.**

Garlic

Why not plant a few cloves of garlic in a pot or window-box in late winter? It is traditional to plant them on the shortest day of the year, but in reality they can be planted as early as mid-autumn through to late winter. The important thing to know is that garlic needs a cold period of at least one month below 50°F (10°C) in order to form bulbs. Without this, it can form a large single bulb instead of separate cloves. Late planting will depend on local conditions.

Only plant garlic that comes from an organic supplier, rather than supermarket bulbs sold for the kitchen. Break up the bulbs and plant individual cloves with the basal plate at the bottom. Any well-draining garden soil will do, but if you only have a patio or balcony, containers of soil or a loam-based compost will do. Plant the cloves vertically 8in (20cm) apart, so just the tips show above the soil surface. Before planting, apply a dressing of sulphate of potash (which is organically acceptable), at the rate of a light handful per square metre of soil.

Organic tip

Potted patio herbs, such as bay, myrtle and French tarragon, will benefit from some winter protection. Bring them indoors, and place them in a sunny window. Also, dig up roots of mint and pot them up in free-draining compost to grow on indoors for fresh leaves through the winter.

Mint

There are many types of mint, but they're all relatively expensive to buy. If you find a friend who has a type of mint you don't have, ask them to take root cuttings in late winter for you. This is the perfect time to do it, when the plants are dormant.

1 Dig around the base of a mint plant. In the case of a containerized plant, just scrape away some soil. Remove three or four healthy roots and put the soil back in place.

▲ **Mint is one of the most frequently grown – and used – herbs, and it can be propagated in winter.**

2 Cut the roots into lengths of around 2–3in (5–7.5cm).

3 Thin roots, such as mint has, can be laid on a tray of cuttings compost. Push them down gently so they are half covered. Water the compost well, and place the cuttings in a polythene bag. Keep them on a windowsill indoors, and pot them up once you can see them growing.

Parsley

Why not raise some parsley from seed in gentle heat. It can be quite a temperamental seed to germinate, but if you follow the instructions on the packet to the letter you should have no problem with it.

Inform

ation

Glossary

Acid
With a pH value below 7; acid soil is deficient in lime and basic minerals.

Algae
Non–flowering microscopic plants, mainly aquatic; the reason for pond water turning green.

Alkaline
With a pH value above 7.

Annual
Plant grown from seed that germinates, flowers, sets seed and dies in one growing year.

Anther
Flower part; part of the stamen containing pollen.

Balled
A flower – particularly in roses – that does not open properly, and rots when still in bud.

Bare-root
Plants sold with their roots bare of soil (ie not growing in a pot or container).

Biennial
A plant that grows from seed and completes its life cycle within two years.

Blanching
Process of withholding light from a plant to prevent the development of chlorophyll, ie turning green.

Bog garden
An area where the soil is permanently damp, either naturally so or artificially created.

Bolting
Premature flower and seed production.

Boss
Cluster of stamens at the centre of the rose flower.

Budding
A form of grafting, where a bud is stripped off one plant (the scion) and grafted on to the rootstock of another.

Butyl
A strong waterproof material made from rubber, usually supplied in sheets or sold by the roll.

Calcicole
Alkaline–loving plant; one that does not tolerate acid conditions.

Calcifuge
Acid–loving plant such as camellia, rhododendron, pieris and heather.

Cold frame
Unheated structure with a glass or plastic cover, used to protect tender plants and seedlings in the colder months.

Companion plant
Plant that has a beneficial effect on another plant growing nearby; the reasons for these expected and presumed benefits are not always understood.

Crown
Basal part of a perennial plant where roots and stems join at soil level, and from where new shoots are produced.

Cultivar
A cultivated plant clearly distinguished by one or more characteristics and which retains these characteristics when propagated; a contraction of 'cultivated variety', and often abbreviated to 'cv' in plant naming.

Dead-heading
The removal of spent flowers or flowerheads.

Deciduous
Plant that loses its leaves at the end of every growing year, and which renews them at the start of the next.

Dieback
Death of shoots, starting from the tips, and as a result of damage or disease.

Dog rose
The common wild rose, *Rosa canina*, found in hedgerows throughout Europe, Asia and North America and Australia.

Double
Referred to in flower terms as a bloom with several layers of petals; usually there would be a minimum of 20 petals. 'Very double' flowers have more than 40 petals.

Double dig
Digging soil to a depth that is equal to the depth of two spade blades (or 'spits').

Drill
Straight furrow made in the soil, usually with a draw hoe or a pointed stick, for sowing seeds in a straight line.

Espalier
Tree (usually a form of fruit tree) trained and tied against a wall, fence or wire support, as a main vertical stem with three or more tiers of branches horizontally in pairs on either side.

Evergreen
Plants that keep their leaves all year round; note that some older leaves are lost regardless of the time of year.

Fan
Tree or bush (usually a form of fruiting plant) trained against a wall, fence or wire support, in the shape of a fan.

Forcing
Making a plant grow, flower or fruit before its natural season, usually carried out by increasing the localized temperature and/or lighting.

Genus (*pl.* **Genera**)
A category in plant naming, comprising a group of related species.

Germination
When a seed starts to grow, by producing a small root and shoot.

Graft
Method of propagation by which an artificial union is made between a shoot or bud of one plant, and the rootstock of another so that they eventually function as one plant.

Graft union (*or* **Union**)
The point at which the scion and rootstock are joined.

Ground cover
Usually low–growing plants that grow over the soil, so suppressing weed growth.

Half-hardy
Plants that are likely not to survive severe frosts; also referred to as 'tender'.

Hardening off
Acclimatizing plants to outside temperatures and conditions; this typically is done to young seedlings and cuttings that have been grown in artificially warm conditions. Hardening off should be carried out over several weeks.

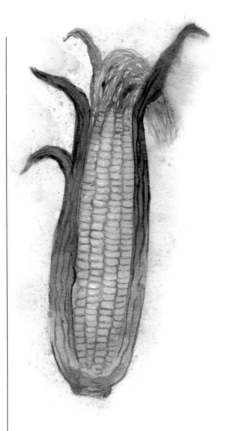

Hardwood cutting
Method of propagation by which a cutting is taken from mature wood at the end of the growing season.

Hardy
Plants that can normally survive frosts.

Heeling in
Laying plants in the soil, with the roots covered, as a temporary measure until full planting can take place.

Herbaceous
Plants (usually) with non-woody stems, that die down at the end of the growing season.

Humus
Organic matter that has been broken down by bacteria in the soil, resulting in a black, crumbly substance from which plants can easily extract life-supporting nutrients.

Hybrid
The offspring of genetically different parents, usually produced in cultivation, but occasionally arising in the wild.

Hybrid Tea
Bush rose producing large flowers, usually single or in very small clusters.

Layering
Type of propagation in which a stem is begged down into the soil (or a pot of growing compost) and encouraged to root, whilst still attached to the parent plant.

Leaching
Loss of nutrients from the topsoil, carried downwards by water (usually rainwater).

Leader
The main, usually central, stem of a plant; also the terminal shoot of a main branch.

Lime
Compounds of calcium; alkaline. This can be used to 'sweeten' an acidic soil, to make it suitable for growing a wider range of plants.

Loam
Type of soil, composed of a reasonably balanced mix of clay, sand and basic nutrients; regarded as the best soil for growing the vast majority of cultivated plants.

Maiden
A one year–old tree.

Marginal plant
Plants that grow partially submerged in shallow water or in boggy soil at the edge a pond or lake.

Mulch
Layer of material applied to the soil surface, to conserve moisture, improve its structure, protect roots from frost and suppress weeds.

Oxygenator
Submerged aquatic plant, the leaves and stems of which release oxygen into the water as a by-product of photosynthesis.

Peat
Partially decayed organic matter. Usually acid, it is used for adding to composts and mulches. For environmental reasons, it is better to use peat substitutes such as coconut fibre or bark.

Perennial
Hardy or tender plant that lives for at least three seasons.

Photosynthesis
The process of food manufacture in plants, whereby chlorophyll in leaves traps the sun's energy, combines it with carbon dioxide in the air and hydrogen in water and creates carbohydrates.

pH scale
A scale measured from 1–14 that indicates the alkalinity or acidity of soil. pH 7 is neutral; pH 1–7 is the acidic range, pH 7–14 is alkaline.

Pinnatisect leaves
Leaves that are divided almost to the midrib at several places.

Pollinate
Transfer of pollen from the anther to the stigma; can be carried out by insects, birds, the wind and by human interaction with the use of brushes, cotton wool buds, etc.

Potash
Form of potassium that is contained in soil and fertilizer, and used by plants.

Pricking out
The transferring of seedlings from the pot, tray or bed in which they germinated, to pots or areas of the garden where they can develop.

Quartered
A characteristic of some roses, particularly the older cultivars, where the flowers are roughly divided into quarters when they open out.

Ray floret
The 'petals' of the flowers of some members of the daisy family.

Recurrent flowering (*see* 'Repeat flowering')

Remontant
A plant that flowers more than once during the growing season.

Repeat (*or* **Recurrent**) **flowering**
The production of two or more flushes during the growing season.

Reverse
The side of the petal that faces away from the centre of the flower.

Rhizome
A specialized, usually horizontally creeping, swollen or slender underground stem that acts as a storage organ, producing shoots along its length.

Rootball
The roots and surrounding soil or compost visible when a plant is removed from a pot.

Rootstock
A plant used to provide the root system for a grafted plant.

Rosette
Flower shape characterized by radiating circles of petals.

Scion
A shoot or bud cut from one plant to graft on to the rootstock of another.

Scorch
Leaves turning brown and dry as a result of bright sunlight hot weather (also cold winds and chemical spray damage).

Seedling
A young plant that has developed, accidentally or intentionally, from a seed.

Self-fertile
A plant that does not need another plant of the same type planted nearby for pollination.

Self-sterile
A plant that needs another plant of the same type nearby for pollination.

Semi-double
Referred to in flower terms as a bloom with more than a single layer of petals; usually there would be 10–20 petals.

Side shoot
A stem that arises from the side of a main shoot or stem.

Single
In flower terms, a single layer of petals opening out into a fairly flat shape, comprising no more than five petals.

Spathe
A large leaf–like structure that encloses or surrounds the flower of certain plants, such as those of the Arum family.

Species
A category in plant naming, the rank below genus, containing related, individual plants.

Sport
A mutation, caused by a genetic change (accidental or intentional) which may produced shoots with different characteristics, such as flowers with a different colour.

Spur
Slow–growing short branch system on fruit trees, usually carrying clusters of fruit buds.

Stamen(s)
The male flower organ, which carries an anther (or anthers) that produce(s) pollen.

Stigma
Flower part; pollen–receiving female organ.

Stomata
Microscopic pores on the undersides of leaves. They control the water content of the plant by opening, to allow transpiration, and closing to prevent it.

Sub-shrub
A plant that produces some woody mature growth, but the soft growth of which will die down in winter.

Sucker
Generally a shoot that arises from below ground, emanating from a plant's roots, but also refers to any shoot on a grafted plant that originates from below the graft union.

Topsoil
The fertile, uppermost layer of soil.

Transpiration
Part of the natural process of photosynthesis whereby plants lose water through their leaves into the atmosphere. Should the rate of transpiration exceed the rate of water intake via the roots, the plant will dehydrate and start to wilt.

Truss
A compact cluster of blooms, or fruits such as tomatoes; often large and decorative.

Underplanting
Low–growing plants planted beneath larger plants.

Variety
Botanically, a naturally occurring variant of a wild species; usually shorted to 'var' in plant naming.

Wind-rock
Destabilizing of a plant's roots by the wind.

Further reading

Books

Clarke, Graham, *Pruning*
(Collins Practical Gardener, 2005)

Clarke, Graham, *The Organic Herb Gardener*
(GMC Publications, 2010)

Clarke, Graham and Toogood, Alan, *The Complete Book of Plant Propagation* (Ward Lock, 1990)

Cuthbertson, Yvonne, *The Organic Vegetable Gardener* (GMC Publications, 2011)

Cuthbertson, Yvonne, *The Organic Fruit Gardener* (GMC Publications, 2011)

Kitto, Dick, *Planning Your Organic Vegetable Garden* (Thorsons, 1986)

Peel, Lucy, *Kitchen Garden*
(Collins Practical Gardener, 2003)

Purnell, Bob, *Crops in Pots*
(Hamlyn, 2007)

Shepherd, Allan, *The Organic Garden – green gardening for a healthy planet* (Collins, 2007)

Slatcher, Julian, *Success with Wild Flowers and Plants* (GMC Publications, 2006)

Stickland, Sue, *The Organic Garden*
(Hamlyn, 1989)

Organic seed suppliers

These are just a few of the huge selection of organic seed suppliers available.

UK

Chase Organics Ltd
Riverdene Business Park
Molesey Road
Hersham
Surrey
KT12 4RG
tel: +44 (0) 1932 253666
www.organiccatalogue.com
www.chaseorganics.co.uk

HDRA Heritage Seed Library
Garden Organic
Coventry
Warwickshire
CV8 3LG
tel: +44 (0) 2476 303517
www.gardenorganic.org.uk

Tamar Organics
Cartha Martha Farm
Rezare
Launceston
Cornwall
PL15 9NX
tel: +44 (0) 1579 371087
www.tamarorganics.co.uk

Thompson & Morgan (UK) Ltd
Poplar Lane
Ipswich
Suffolk
United Kingdom
IP8 3BU
tel: +44 (0) 844 248 5383
www.thompson-morgan.com

US

Park Seed Company
1 Parkton Avenue
Greenwood
SC 29647
tel: +1 800-213-0076
www.parkseed.com

Peaceful Valley Farm & Garden Supply
P.O. Box 2209
Grass Valley, CA 95945
tel: +1 888-784-1722
www.groworganic.com

Seeds of Change
tel: +1 888-762-7333
www.seedsofchange.com

Thompson & Morgan
P.O. Box 397
Aurora
IN 47001-0397
tel: +1 800-274-7333
www.tmseeds.com

White Flower Farm
P.O. Box 50
Litchfield
Connecticut 06759-0050
tel: +1 800-503-9624
www.whiteflowerfarm.com

Useful websites

American Horticultural Society
www.ahs.org

Centre for Organic Seed Information
www.cosi.org.uk

Garden Organic (HDRA)
www.gardenorganic.org.uk

Institute of Horticulture
www.horticulture.org.uk

National Fruit Collection
www.brogdale.org

National Society of Allotment & Leisure Gardeners
www.nsalg.org.uk

Organic Farmers and Growers
www.organicfarmers.org.uk

Permaculture Association
www.permaculture.org.uk

Primal Seeds
www.primalseeds.org

Royal Horticultural Society (RHS)
www.rhs.org.uk

The Soil Association
www.soilassociation.org

About the author

Graham Clarke is an award–winning writer, who has gardened organically since the birth of his first daughter, in 1990. He was born into gardening – literally. His father was in charge of the world–famous Regent's Park in London and, when Graham appeared, the family lived in a lodge within the gardens there. During his formative years he was surrounded by quality horticulture, so it was little surprise when he chose this as his career.

He went to study with England's Royal Horticultural Society at Wisley Gardens, and after that worked as a gardener at Buckingham Palace in London. This very private garden is seen by Her Majesty the Queen on most of the days she is in residence.

For more than 25 years, Graham has been a gardening writer and journalist. He has written 12 books, and countless articles for most of the major UK gardening magazines. At various times he was editor of *Amateur Gardening* (the UK's leading weekly magazine for amateurs) and *Horticulture Week* (the UK's leading weekly magazine for professionals). He writes for *Healthy & Organic Living*, and wrote a column in every issue of its predecessor, *Organic Life*.

Graham lives in Dorset, on England's south coast, with his wife and two daughters. Here the air is clear, with distinctly reduced levels of lead and carbon monoxide – which makes gardening organically not just easier, but more pleasurable.

Index

To place an order, or to request a catalogue, contact:
GMC Publications
Castle Place, 166 High Street, Lewes, East Sussex, BN7 1XU
United Kingdom
Tel: +44 (0)1273 488005 Fax: +44 (0)1273 402866
Website: www.gmcbooks.com
Orders by credit card are accepted